Managing Editor
Mara Ellen Guckian

Editors in Chief
Karen J. Goldfluss, M.S. Ed.
Ina Massler Levin, M.A.

Cover Artist
Diem Pascarella

Creative Director
Karen J. Goldfluss, M.S. Ed.

Art Coordinator
Renée Mc Elwee

Illustrator
Mark Mason

Imaging
James Edward Grace
Craig Gunnell
Rosa C. See

Publisher
Mary D. Smith, M.S. Ed.

TCR 2610

CORRELATED TO COMMON CORE STANDARDS

Instant Math Practice

Standards-based exercises for year-round practice!

- Number and Operations
- Algebra
- Geometry
- Measurement and Data
- Problem Solving

Teacher Created Resources

Written and Compiled by
Mara Ellen Guckian

The classroom teacher may reproduce the materials in this book and/or CD for use in a single classroom only. The reproduction of any part of this book and/or CD for other classrooms or for an entire school or school system is strictly prohibited. No part of this publication may be transmitted or recorded in any form without written permission from the publisher with the exception of electronic material, which may be stored on the purchaser's computer only.

Teacher Created Resources
6421 Industry Way
Westminster, CA 92683
www.teachercreated.com
ISBN: 978-1-4206-2610-0

© 2013 Teacher Created Resources
Made in U.S.A.

Teacher Created Resources

Table of Contents

Introduction

The *Instant Math Practice* series was developed to support classroom math curriculums and to provide students with opportunities to master and retain important math skills. Each page was designed to encourage students to discover mathematical relationships and to recognize the value of math in everyday life.

The standards-based pages can be used in whole-class situations to reinforce new concepts being taught. They can also be used in centers to provide additional practice as needed, or for more specific one-on-one RTI (Response to Intervention) support. This series challenges students to think about math, not just memorize facts.

The units are scaffolded to build upon prior knowledge. Each practice page focuses on specific math skills. *Instant Math Practice: Grade 2* includes the following topics:

- **Number Sense** → 0–1,000
- **Addition** → 2- and 3-Digit Numbers; regrouping
- **Subtraction** → 2- and 3-Digit Numbers; regrouping
- **Repeat Addition/Multiplication** → 2s, 3s, 5s, 10s
- **Fractions** → $\frac{1}{2} - \frac{1}{12}$
- **Money** → Coins and Dollars
- **Measurement** → Length, Width, Height, Weight
- **Time** → Calendar, Clocks
- **Geometry** → 2-D and 3-D Shapes, Perimeters

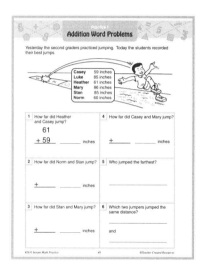

Number and word problems are presented in a variety of ways and incorporate important math vocabulary. The more math vocabulary is incorporated into daily language, the more students will internalize the math they are learning. A broad knowledge of math vocabulary also benefits students during testing.

As active learners working each page, students will develop a strong understanding of grade-level math concepts. And as students progress, their problem-solving skills will improve in math and across other curriculum areas, thus boosting their overall confidence and abilities to learn.

Common Core State Correlations (CCSS)

Correlations have been provided for the Common Core State Standards for Math. For quick viewing of the math correlations, a chart is provided on pages 5 and 6 of this book. (*Note:* This version does not contain page titles but does reference the page numbers.) These charts correlate student page activities to applicable standards within a given domain. For a printable PDF version of the CCSS correlations chart, go to *www.teachercreated.com/standards/*.

Math Vocabulary

- ❏ add
- ❏ addend
- ❏ after
- ❏ all together
- ❏ amount
- ❏ base
- ❏ before
- ❏ between
- ❏ borrow
- ❏ circle
- ❏ color
- ❏ column
- ❏ compare
- ❏ copy
- ❏ corner
- ❏ correct
- ❏ count
- ❏ curve
- ❏ cut
- ❏ denominator
- ❏ difference
- ❏ digit
- ❏ divide

- ❏ draw
- ❏ equal
- ❏ estimate
- ❏ face
- ❏ fewer
- ❏ fraction
- ❏ geometry
- ❏ graph
- ❏ greater
- ❏ half (halves)
- ❏ hexagon
- ❏ horizontal
- ❏ left
- ❏ less
- ❏ match
- ❏ measure
- ❏ minus
- ❏ more
- ❏ multiply
- ❏ number
- ❏ numerator
- ❏ operation
- ❏ pairs

- ❏ perimeter
- ❏ plus
- ❏ product
- ❏ quarter
- ❏ read
- ❏ rectangle
- ❏ regroup
- ❏ rhombus
- ❏ right
- ❏ row
- ❏ same
- ❏ set
- ❏ shaded
- ❏ side
- ❏ solve
- ❏ square
- ❏ subtract
- ❏ sum
- ❏ symmetry
- ❏ tally
- ❏ third
- ❏ triangle
- ❏ vertical

Common Core State Standards Correlation

Student practice pages in *Instant Math Practice* have been correlated the following Common Core State Standards © Copyright 2010. National Governors Association Center for Best Practices and Council of Chief State School Officers. All rights reserved. For more information about the Common Core State Standards, go to *http://www.corestandards.org/*.

Mathematics Standards	Page
Operations & Algebraic Thinking	
Represent and solve problems involving addition and subtraction.	
2.OA.1. Use addition and subtraction within 100 to solve one- and two-step word problems involving situations of adding to, taking from, putting together, taking apart, and comparing, with unknowns in all positions, e.g., by using drawings and equations with a symbol for the unknown number to represent the problem.	14, 16, 48, 49, 60, 61, 82, 83, 109, 110, 111, 112, 114
Add and subtract within 20.	
2.OA.2. Fluently add and subtract within 20 using mental strategies. By end of Grade 2, know from memory all sums of two one-digit numbers.	13, 14, 15, 16, 50, 51
Work with equal groups of objects to gain foundations for multiplication.	
2.OA.3. Determine whether a group of objects (up to 20) has an odd or even number of members, e.g., by pairing objects or counting them by 2s; write an equation to express an even number as a sum of two equal addends.	62, 63, 64, 65, 66
2.OA.4. Use addition to find the total number of objects arranged in rectangular arrays with up to 5 rows and up to 5 columns; write an equation to express the total as a sum of equal addends.	32, 70, 77, 78, 79, 82, 83
Number & Operations in Base Ten	
Understand place value.	
2.NBT.1. Understand that the three digits of a three-digit number represent amounts of hundreds, tens, and ones; e.g., 706 equals 7 hundreds, 0 tens, and 6 ones.	19, 20, 21, 22, 23, 24, 25, 26, 27, 30, 33, 34, 35, 36
2.NBT.2. Count within 1000; skip-count by 5s, 10s, and 100s.	15, 18, 65, 66, 67, 68, 69, 70, 71, 72, 73, 74, 75, 77, 78, 79, 82, 83, 109
2.NBT.3. Read and write numbers to 1000 using base-ten numerals, number names, and expanded form.	16, 17, 18, 19, 20, 22, 31, 32, 33, 34, 35, 36
2.NBT.4. Compare two three-digit numbers based on meanings of the hundreds, tens, and ones digits, using >, =, and < symbols to record the results of comparisons.	21, 23, 24, 25, 26, 27, 28, 29, 30, 32
Use place value understanding and properties of operations to add and subtract.	
2.NBT.5. Fluently add and subtract within 100 using strategies based on place value, properties of operations, and/or the relationship between addition and subtraction.	37, 38, 39, 40, 41, 42, 43, 48, 49, 50, 51, 52, 53, 54, 60, 61
2.NBT.6. Add up to four two-digit numbers using strategies based on place value and properties of operations.	38, 39, 40, 41, 42, 43, 44, 45, 46, 47

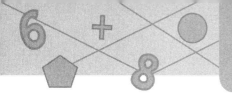
Number & Operations in Base Ten *(Cont.)*	
2.NBT.7. Add and subtract within 1000, using concrete models or drawings and strategies based on place value, properties of operations, and/or the relationship between addition and subtraction; relate the strategy to a written method. Understand that in adding or subtracting three-digit numbers, one adds or subtracts hundreds and hundreds, tens and tens, ones and ones; and sometimes it is necessary to compose or decompose tens or hundreds.	46, 47, 55, 56, 57, 58, 59, 60, 61
2.NBT.8. Mentally add 10 or 100 to a given number 100–900, and mentally subtract 10 or 100 from a given number 100–900.	77, 78, 79, 80, 81
2.NBT.9. Explain why addition and subtraction strategies work, using place value and the properties of operations.	37, 38, 39, 40, 41, 42, 43, 48, 49, 50, 51, 52, 53, 54, 55, 56, 60, 61

Measurement & Data	
Measure and estimate lengths in standard units.	
2.MD.1. Measure the length of an object by selecting and using appropriate tools such as rulers, yardsticks, meter sticks, and measuring tapes.	102, 104, 105, 106
2.MD.2. Measure the length of an object twice, using length units of different lengths for the two measurements; describe how the two measurements relate to the size of the unit chosen.	102, 104, 105, 106
2.MD.3. Estimate lengths using units of inches, feet, centimeters, and meters.	104
2.MD.4. Measure to determine how much longer one object is than another, expressing the length difference in terms of a standard length unit.	102, 107
Relate addition and subtraction to length.	
2.MD.5. Use addition and subtraction within 100 to solve word problems involving lengths that are given in the same units, e.g., by using drawings (such as drawings of rulers) and equations with a symbol for the unknown number to represent the problem.	104, 105, 106, 107, 108, 129, 130, 131, 132
2.MD.6. Represent whole numbers as lengths from 0 on a number line diagram with equally spaced points corresponding to the numbers 0, 1, 2, ..., and represent whole-number sums and differences within 100 on a number line diagram.	80, 107, 108
Work with time and money.	
2.MD.7. Tell and write time from analog and digital clocks to the nearest five minutes, using a.m. and p.m.	115, 116, 117, 118, 119, 120, 121, 122, 123
2.MD.8. Solve word problems involving dollar bills, quarters, dimes, nickels, and pennies, using $ and ¢ symbols appropriately. Example: If you have 2 dimes and 3 pennies, how many cents do you have?	23, 96, 97, 98, 99, 100, 101
Represent and interpret data.	
2.MD.10. Draw a picture graph and a bar graph (with single-unit scale) to represent a data set with up to four categories. Solve simple put-together, take-apart, and compare problems using information presented in a bar graph.	7, 8, 9

Geometry	
Reason with shapes and their attributes.	
2.G.1. Recognize and draw shapes having specified attributes, such as a given number of angles or a given number of equal faces. Identify triangles, quadrilaterals, pentagons, hexagons, and cubes.	7, 38, 58, 69, 85, 124, 125, 126, 127, 128, 129, 130, 131, 132

Use tally marks to show the number of items in each box. Graph your findings.

Tally Marks →		= 1	|| = 2	||| = 3	|||| = 4	ⅢⅢ = 5

Items	Tally

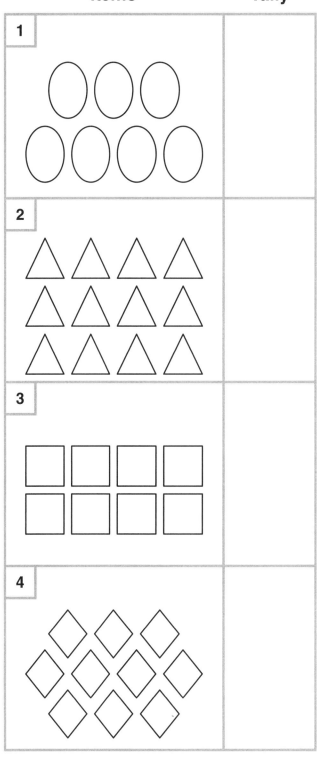

Ovals	Triangles	Squares	Rhombi

Look at the pet shop display. Fill in one column on the graph for each pet.

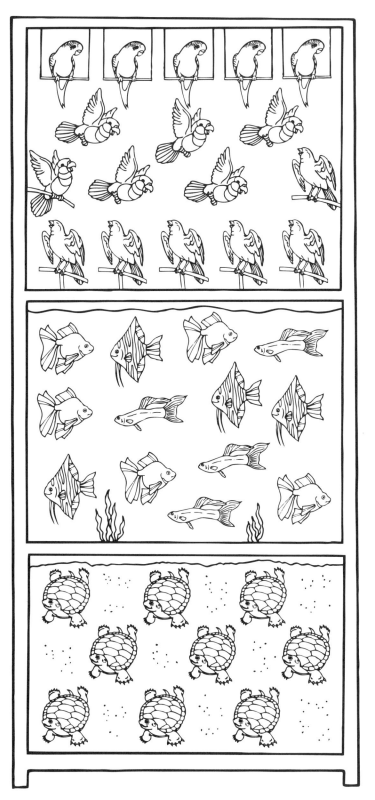

			20
			19
			18
			17
			16
			15
			14
			13
			12
			11
			10
			9
			8
			7
			6
			5
			4
			3
			2
			1
Birds	Fish	Turtles	

How many birds? _____ **How many fish?** _____ **How many turtles?** _____

Charts and Graphs

Look at the chart. The class voted on the vehicles they would like to ride in.

Speedboat	Airplane	Race Car	Hot Air Balloon

1. How many students chose a speedboat? _____

2. How many students chose an airplane? _____

3. How many students chose a race car? _____

4. How many students chose a hot air balloon? _____

5. How many students chose a vehicle that travels in the sky? _____

6. Add your vote.

7. Did it change the outcome for the most popular vehicle?   **Yes   No**

Ordinal Numbers

Follow the directions for each row.

1 Color the *first* item green. Color the *seventh* item yellow.

2 Color the *third* item blue. Color the *sixth* item orange.

3 Color the *second* item red. Color the *fifth* item purple.

4 Color the *fourth* animal pink. Color the *last* animal brown.

10 ©Teacher Created Resources

Cut out the six pictures below. Arrange them in order and glue them to a large sheet of paper. Use the words **first**, **second**, **third**, **fourth**, **fifth**, and **sixth** to label the pictures.

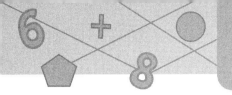

Ordinal Numbers

There are six cars in the race.

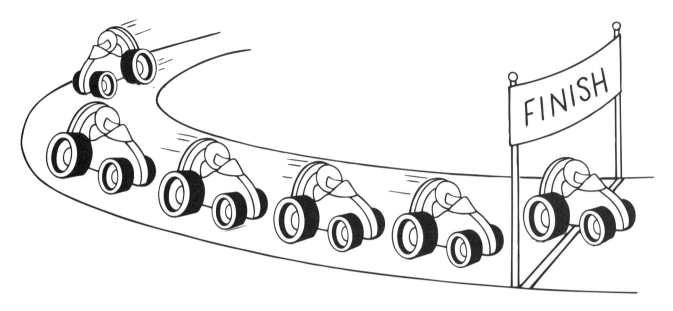

1 Color the car in *last* place blue.

2 Color the car in *second* place red.

3 Color the car in *third* place green.

4 Color the car in *fourth* place yellow.

5 Color the winning car purple.

6 Color the *fifth* car orange.

Draw a line from the car to its position in the race.

7 orange race car		**1st**
8 blue race car		**2nd**
9 red race car		**3rd**
10 green race car		**4th**
11 purple race car		**5th**
12 yellow race car		**6th**

Adding Doubles

Count the spots on the left wing of each ladybug. Draw an equal number of spots on the right wing. Add the spots on both wings to find the total.

1	2	3

_____ + _____ = _____	_____ + _____ = _____	_____ + _____ = _____
4	5	6

_____ + _____ = _____	_____ + _____ = _____	_____ + _____ = _____

Solve each doubles problem.

7   5 + 5 = _____

8   3 + 3 = _____

9   4 + 4 = _____

10   7 + 7 = _____

11   10 + 10 = _____

12   6 + 6 = _____

13   9 + 9 = _____

14   8 + 8 = _____

Adding Doubles

Fill in the blanks to complete each problem.

1 _____ + 7 = 14

2 5 + _____ = 10

3 _____ + 4 = 8

4 6 + _____ = 12

5 _____ + 3 = 6

6 8 + _____ = 16

7 _____ + 9 = 18

8 2 + _____ = 4

9 10 + 10 = _____

10 11 + _____ = 22

11 Josh jumped seven feet. Then he jumped seven more feet. How far did he jump all together?

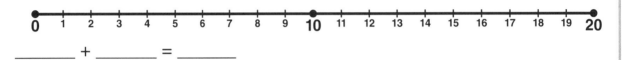

_____ + _____ = _____

12 Sam made four cookies and Dave made four cookies. They put all the cookies on a plate for Dad. How many cookies are on the plate?

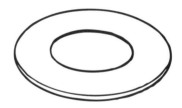

_____ + _____ = _____

13 The team had three balls and the coach brought three more balls to practice. How many balls did they have?

_____ + _____ = _____

14 Grandma and Grandpa each brought a bundle of eight balloons to the picnic. How many balloons were there all together?

_____ + _____ = _____

Tens and Ones

Look at the shapes in each row. Circle groups of ten and draw a rectangle around the shapes left over.

1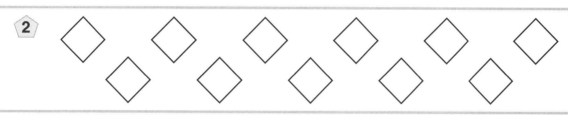

2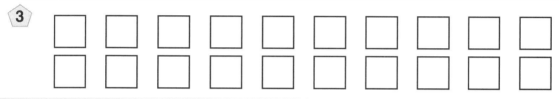

3

Answer the questions below to complete the statements for tens and ones.

4 17 is made up of _____ ten and _____ ones.

5 12 is made up of _____ ten and _____ ones.

6 24 is made up of _____ tens and _____ ones.

7 50 is made up of _____ tens and _____ ones.

8 78 is made up of _____ tens and _____ ones.

9 94 is made up of _____ tens and _____ ones.

Solve the problems and fill in the chart on the right.

Tens	Ones

10 $7 + 9 =$ _____

11 $4 + 7 =$ _____

12 $9 + 5 =$ _____

13 $10 + 9 =$ _____

Add the numbers to find the sums. Then fill in the blanks to show how many *tens* and how many *ones*. The first one has been done for you.

1 7 + 8 = __15__

__15__ has __1__ in the tens place and __5__ in the ones place.

2 22 + 2 = _____

_____ has _____ in the tens place and _____ in the ones place.

3 11 + 8 = _____

_____ has _____ in the tens place and _____ in the ones place.

4 13 + 3 = _____

_____ has _____ in the tens place and _____ in the ones place.

5 7 + 6 = _____

_____ has _____ in the tens place and _____ in the ones place.

6 9 + 5 = _____

_____ has _____ in the tens place and _____ in the ones place.

7 35 + 2 = _____

_____ has _____ in the tens place and _____ in the ones place.

Find the missing number in each horizontal addition equation.

8 12 + _____ = 15   What number in the sum is in the *tens* place? _____

9 15 + _____ = 20   What number in the sum is in the *ones* place? _____

10 | Sandy had twelve round beads. She went to the store and bought eight more. Write the problem.

How many beads did she have in all? _____

Tens and Ones

Fill in the boxes for tens and ones.

1 49 is made up of ☐ tens and ☐ ones.

2 12 is made up of ☐ ten and ☐ ones.

3 24 is made up of ☐ tens and ☐ ones.

4 50 is made up of ☐ tens and ☐ ones.

Solve the problems. Then use the sums to answer the questions.

5 12 + _____ = 15   What number is in the *tens* place? _____

6 11 + _____ = 41   What number is in the *ones* place? _____

7 20 + _____ = 25   What number is in the *tens* place? _____

8 45 – _____ = 40   What number is in the *tens* place? _____

9 60 – _____ = 40   What number is in the *ones* place? _____

10 What number has a two in the *tens* place and a zero in the *ones* place?

11 What number has a nine in the *tens* place and a seven in the *ones* place?

12 What number has a four in the *tens* place and a four in the *ones* place?

13 What number has a six in the *tens* place and an eight in the *ones* place?

What number is represented by each set shown below

1

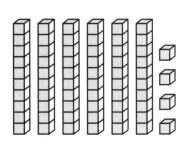

_____ tens _____ ones = _____

2

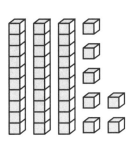

_____ tens _____ ones = _____

3

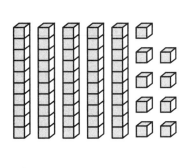

_____ tens _____ ones = _____

4

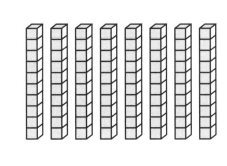

_____ tens _____ ones = _____

5 Use number words to write the sums. Don't forget the hyphens!

twenty and seven _____

forty and nine _____

ten and ten _____

thirty and five _____

6 Circle the bars and unit cubes needed to show 77.

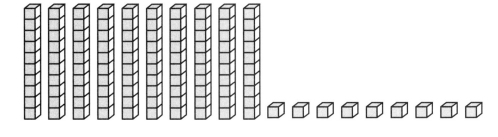

Hundreds

Look at the numbers in the "spots" on the dog and answer the questions below. Write the answers in the bones.

1 Which number has a four in the *hundreds* place?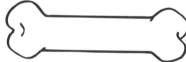

2 Which number has an eight in the *ones* place?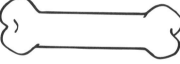

3 Which number has a five in the *tens* place?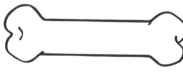

4 Which number has a two in the *hundreds* place?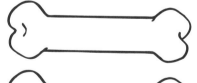

5 Which number has a six in the *ones* place?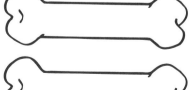

6 Which number has an eight in the *tens* place?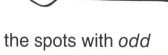

7 Color the spots with *even* numbers brown. Color the spots with *odd* numbers black.

Hundreds

Fill in the chart for each number to show how many *hundreds*, *tens*, and *ones*.

		Hundreds	Tens	Ones
1	176			
2	398			
3	479			
4	582			
5	870			
6	285			
7	902			
8	747			
9	891			

Add the numbers to find the sums. Then fill in the blanks to show how many *hundreds*, *tens*, and *ones* in each answer.

100 + 50 + 8 = 158

<u>1</u> in the *hundreds* place, <u>5</u> in the *tens* place, and <u>8</u> in the *ones* place.

10	200 + 50 + 3 = _____
	_____ in the *hundreds* place, _____ in the *tens* place, and _____ in the *ones* place.
11	330 + 30 = _____
	_____ in the *hundreds* place, _____ in the *tens* place, and _____ in the *ones* place.
12	500 + 13 = _____
	_____ in the *hundreds* place, _____ in the *tens* place, and _____ in the *ones* place.

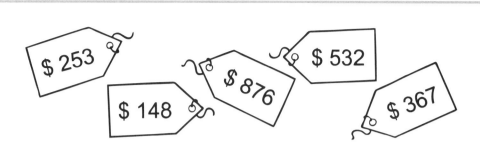

1 Which price tag has a three in the *hundreds* spot? _____

2 Which price tag has an eight in the *ones* spot? _____

3 Which price tag has a five in the *tens* spot? _____

4 Which price tag has a two in the *ones* spot? _____

5 Which price tag has a six in the *ones* spot? _____

Look below at the prices of the items for sale. Answer questions 6 and 7.

6 How much is the *most* expensive item? _____

7 How much is the *least* expensive item? _____

How many *hundreds*, *tens*, and *ones* are shown in each row?

1

_____ hundreds _____ tens _____ ones

2

_____ hundreds _____ tens _____ ones

3

_____ hundreds _____ tens _____ ones

4

_____ hundreds _____ tens _____ ones

Least to Greatest

Arrange the numbers in each row from *least* (smallest) to *greatest* (largest).

1

100	10	110	101	1
_____	_____	_____	_____	_____

2

220	202	230	23	32
_____	_____	_____	_____	_____

3

35	533	353	350	53
_____	_____	_____	_____	_____

4

The fee for each cab ride is shown on top of the cab. Arrange the fees from least to greatest.

least _____ _____ _____ _____ **greatest**

Look at the numbers in each row. Write them in order from *least* to *greatest*.

1 459   951   876   _____ _____ _____

2 976   796   679   _____ _____ _____

3 456   457   455   _____ _____ _____

4 600   400   900   _____ _____ _____

5 215   512   152   _____ _____ _____

Arrange the five numbers in each row below from *least* to *greatest*.

6 **980**   **789**   **687**   **899**   **779**

_____   _____   _____   _____   _____

7 **443**   **344**   **345**   **354**   **305**

_____   _____   _____   _____   _____

8 Annie is 40 years old. Her son is 12 years old and her daughter is 22 years old. Arrange the ages in order from youngest to oldest.

_____ _____ _____

9 Tristan has 320 pennies. His uncle has 450 pennies and his dad has 540 pennies. His older brother has 230 pennies.

Arrange the pennies in order from least to most.

_____   _____   _____   _____

Look at the numbers in each mitt. Arrange the numbers to create the *least* number possible. Write that number on the ball on the left. Write the *greatest* number you can make in the bat in the right column. The first one has been done.

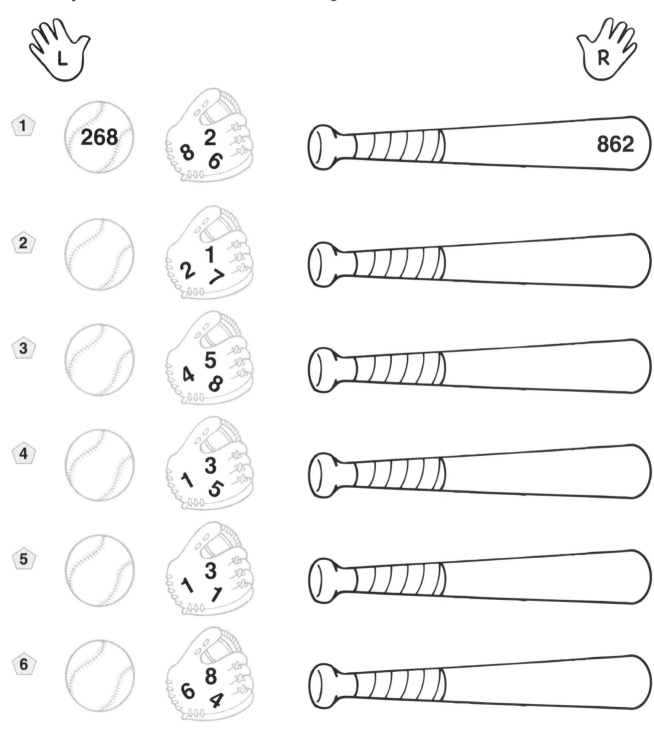

L ... **R**

1. 268 — [2 8 6] ... 862

2. [1 2 7]

3. [5 4 8]

4. [3 1 5]

5. [3 1 1]

6. [8 6 4]

7. Circle the *least* number in the column on the left. _____

8. Circle the *greatest* number in the column on the right. _____

Greater Than, Less Than

Use the "greater than" sign **(>)** or the "less than" sign **(<)** to compare the numbers below. The first one has been done for you.

Write the letter **G** in the circle over the number that is *greater* in each problem.

Write the letter **L** in the circle over the number that is *less*.

1
(L)   (G)

230 **<** 320

5
( )   ( )

102   100

2
( )   ( )

180   810

6
( )   ( )

260   270

3
( )   ( )

450   412

7
( )   ( )

762   626

4
( )   ( )

300   400

8
( )   ( )

171   117

9   Draw a school of fish that shows less than 10 fish. Fill in the statement.

<   _____ < _____

Look at the "greater than" sign **(>)** or the "less than" sign **(<)** to compare the numbers below. If the statement is *true*, put a **T** on the line. If the statement is *false*, put an **F** on the line.

1   10 > 22 _____

2   6 < 9 _____

3   15 > 51 _____

4   23 < 43 _____

5   55 > 32 _____

6   21 < 12 _____

7   87 > 78 _____

8   19 < 28 _____

9   21 > 22 _____

10   10 < 9 _____

Fill in the oval with the correct symbol (> or <) for each statement.

11   39 ⬭ 22

12   48 ⬭ 54

13   90 ⬭ 67

14   77 ⬭ 89

15   42 ⬭ 98

16   198 ⬭ 89

17   100 ⬭ 180

18   123 ⬭ 232

19   700 ⬭ 800

20   265 ⬭ 252

Answer the word problems. Write an equation using the "greater than" sign **(>)** or the "less than" sign **(<)** to compare each set of numbers.

1 Jane has one dozen eggs and Eric has 10 eggs.

Who has more eggs? _____

_____ ( ) _____

2 Tai has two bags of marbles and each bag has five marbles in it. How many marbles does Tai have? _____

Jacob has nine marbles in his bag.

Who has more marbles? _____

_____ ( ) _____

3 Sara has fifty chickens in her backyard. Her uncle has fifteen chickens.

Who has more chickens? _____

_____ ( ) _____

4 There were twelve buses parked on the lot on Tuesday. There were twenty-two buses parked on the lot on Thursday.

Which day had more busses on the lot? _____

_____ ( ) _____

Greater, Less, Equal

Use the "greater than" sign **(>)**, the "less than" sign **(<)**, or the "equal" sign **(=)** to complete each comparison.

1 21 $\bigcirc$ 12   **6** 33 $\bigcirc$ 49

2 32 $\bigcirc$ 34   **7** 21 $\bigcirc$ 21

3 25 $\bigcirc$ 15   **8** 40 $\bigcirc$ 49

4 45 $\bigcirc$ 50   **9** 38 $\bigcirc$ 38

5 39 $\bigcirc$ 29   **10** 50 $\bigcirc$ 30

Read each statement. Rewrite the statement using a **>**, **<** or **=** sign. Answer the question in each box.

---

11 | Jake has three bats and Jenny has four bats.

_____ $\bigcirc$ _____

Who has more bats? _____

---

12 | Sam has 14 model airplanes and Seth has 40.

_____ $\bigcirc$ _____

Who has more airplanes? _____

---

13 | My mom has a dozen dresses and my sister Emma has 12.

_____ $\bigcirc$ _____

Who has more dresses? _____

Greater, Less, Equal

Use the "greater than" sign **(>)**, the "less than" sign **(<)**, or the "equal" sign **(=)** to complete each comparison.

1. 211 ⬭ 112

2. 320 ⬭ 340

3. 245 ⬭ 415

4. 848 ⬭ 958

5. 639 ⬭ 692

6. 303 ⬭ 409

7. 821 ⬭ 281

8. 409 ⬭ 409

9. 138 ⬭ 318

10. 500 ⬭ 390

Look at the "greater than" **(>)**, less than **(<)**, or "equal" **(=)** signs to compare the numbers below. If the statement is *true*, put a **T** on the line next to it. If the statement is *false*, put an **F** on the line next to it.

11. 710 > 272 _____   _____

12. 609 < 960 _____   _____

13. 415 > 541 _____   _____

14. 423 < 43 _____   _____

15. 545 = 545 _____   _____

16. 21 = 12 _____   _____

17. 870 > 780 _____   _____

18. 819 < 828 _____   _____

19. 210 = 212 _____   _____

20. 10 < 9 _____   _____

Correct the number statements that are *false*. Write the correct statement on the line provided.

Write the following as numbers:

1 twenty-eight _____

2 thirty-nine _____

3 eleven _____

4 forty-six _____

5 twenty-four _____

6 sixteen _____

7 nine _____

8 fifteen _____

9 fifty _____

10 forty-four _____

Write the correct number word next to each number.

11 18 _____

12 12 _____

13 36 _____

14 17 _____

15 23 _____

16 34 _____

17 7 _____

18 49 _____

19 33 _____

20 42 _____

Use the correct sign (**>, <, =**) in each problem.

1   13 ⬭ thirty-one   **6**   twenty-nine ⬭ 49

2   43 ⬭ forty-three   **7**   forty-eight ⬭ 28

3   22 ⬭ twenty-three   **8**   sixteen ⬭ 16

4   50 ⬭ forty-eight   **9**   thirty-two ⬭ 42

5   33 ⬭ thirty   **10**   eighteen ⬭ 17

Count the stars. Write the numbers and number words for the totals.

11

Number _____   **Number Word** _____

12

Number _____   **Number Word** _____

Number Words 1–100

Draw a line from each number word in the column on the left to its number in the column on the right.

L			R
1	fifty-seven		79
2	thirty-eight		99
3	eighteen		57
4	seventy-nine		100
5	ninety-nine		82
6	ninety-four		94
7	eighty-two		18
8	twenty-six		26
9	one hundred		38

10 Count the *hundreds*, *tens*, and *ones*. Circle the number words below that show the total number of cubes.

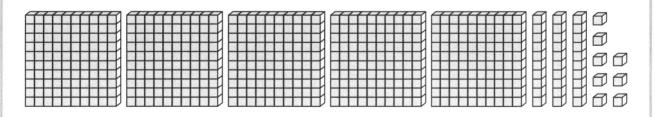

six hundred thirty-five   **three hundred thirty-six**   **five hundred thirty-eight**

Number Words 1–100

Draw a line from each number in the column on the left to its number word in the column on the right.

1 75		ninety-seven
2 83		one hundred
3 13		thirteen
4 97		seventy-two
5 100		sixty-one
6 72		eighty-three
7 49		seventy-five
8 28		twenty-eight
9 61		forty-nine

10

Count the *hundreds*, *tens,* and *ones*. Circle the number words below that show the total.

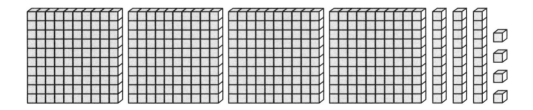

four hundred forty-three   **four hundred thirty-four**   **four hundred fifty-four**

Number Words 1–1,000

Write the following as numbers:

1 two hundred twenty-eight   _____

2 one hundred ninety-nine   _____

3 seven hundred eleven   _____

4 five hundred fifty-six   _____

5 three hundred sixty-four   _____

6 one thousand   _____

Match the following numbers on the left to the correct number words in the column to the right.

7 718   one thousand

8 1,000   seven hundred eighteen

9 894   eight hundred ninety-four

10 526   six hundred forty-nine

11 984   nine hundred eighty-four

12 649   five hundred twenty-six

Number Words 1–1,000

Write each number word as a number. Then draw a line to the number in the column on the right that comes *after* the number in the column on the left.

L

R

1 nine hundred ninety-nine _____   350

2 six hundred twenty-two _____   639

3 three hundred forty-nine _____   1000

4 three hundred twenty-two_____   949

5 nine hundred forty-eight _____   323

6 six hundred thirty-eight_____   623

Use number words to write the following numbers.

7 1000 _____

8 477 _____

9 692 _____

10 835 _____

11 922 _____

12 546 _____

Adding 2-Digit Numbers

Help solve the mystery. Find the sums and follow the directions below.

1 21 +18	**2** 31 +16	**3** 31 +21
4 46 +31	**5** 12 +12	**6** 21 +28

It is not 24. Cross it out.

It is not 39. Cross it out.

It is not 52. Cross it out.

It is not 77. Cross it out.

It is not 47. Cross it out.

7. What is the secret number? _____

Adding 2-Digit Numbers

Solve the problem in each shape to find the sum. Use the word bank at the bottom to label the shape on the line below it.

1

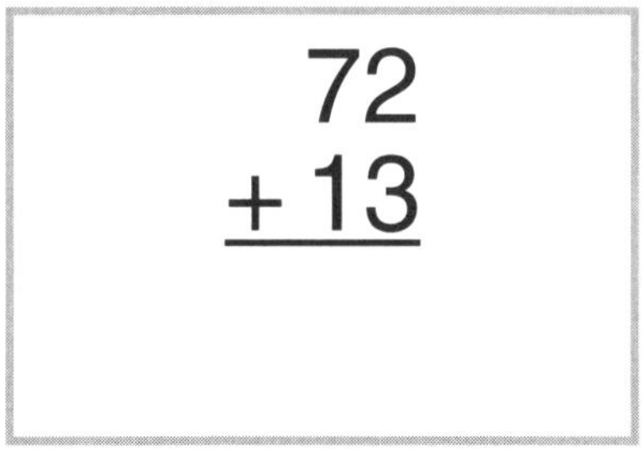

$$72$$
$$+13$$

_____

2

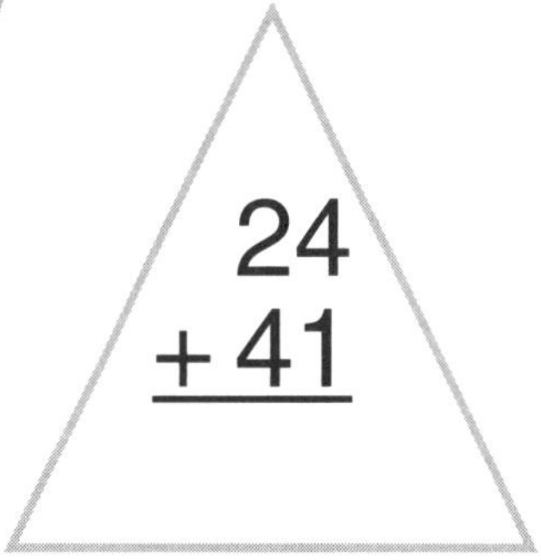

$$24$$
$$+41$$

_____

3

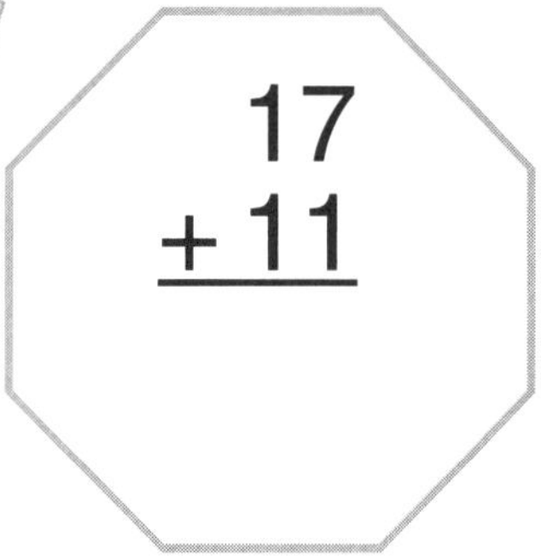

$$17$$
$$+11$$

_____

4

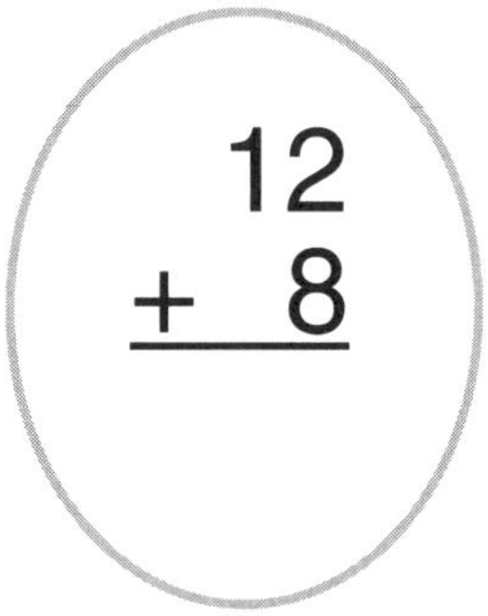

$$12$$
$$+\ 8$$

_____

5

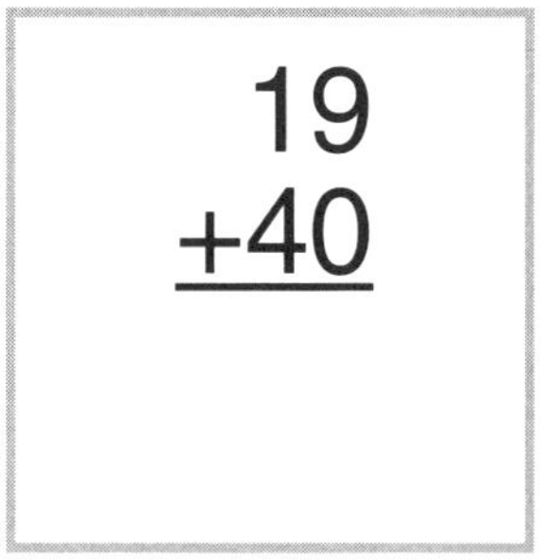

$$19$$
$$+40$$

_____

6

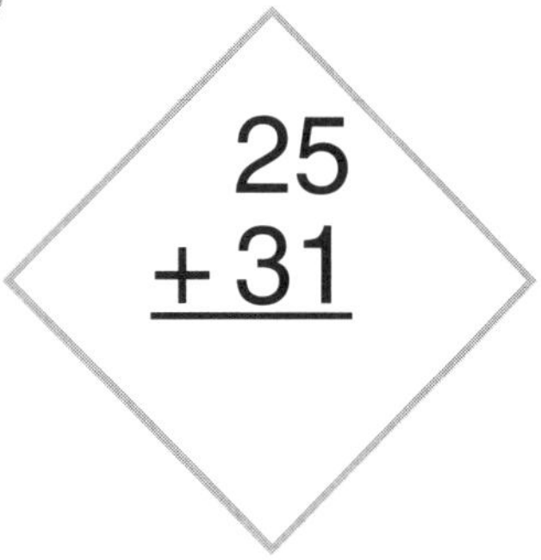

$$25$$
$$+31$$

_____

7

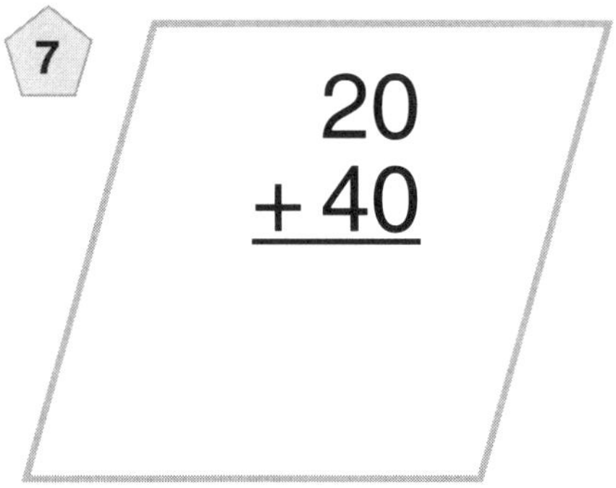

$$20$$
$$+40$$

_____

8

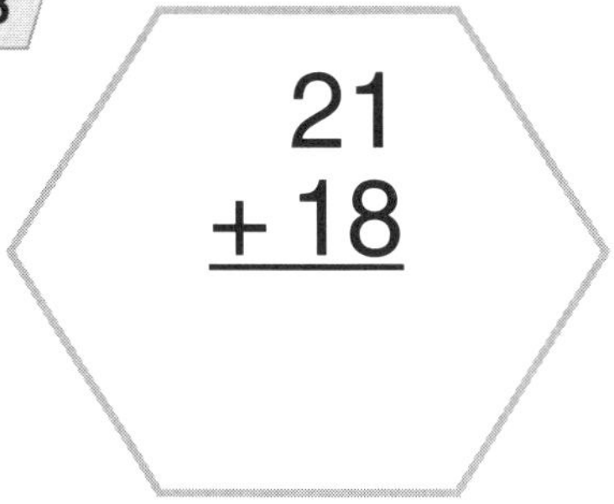

$$21$$
$$+18$$

_____

9

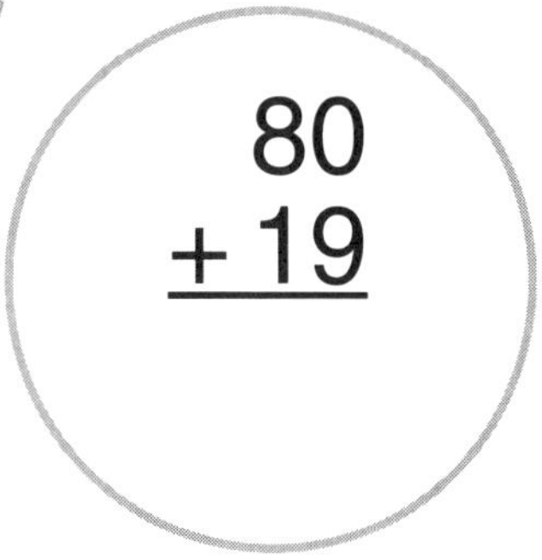

$$80$$
$$+19$$

_____

Word Bank	rectangle	square	circle
	oval	rhombus	triangle
	parallelogram	hexagon	octagon

Adding 2-Digit Numbers

Solve the addition problems.

1
$$17 + 22$$

2
$$54 + 21$$

3
$$76 + 22$$

4
$$18 + 31$$

5
$$70 + 20$$

6
$$11 + 11$$

7
$$51 + 21$$

8
$$19 + 10$$

9
$$62 + 22$$

Use the answers to problems 1–10 to complete the dot-to-dot below. Connect the answer from the first problem to the answer to the second problem. Keep connecting the answers in the order the problems are given.

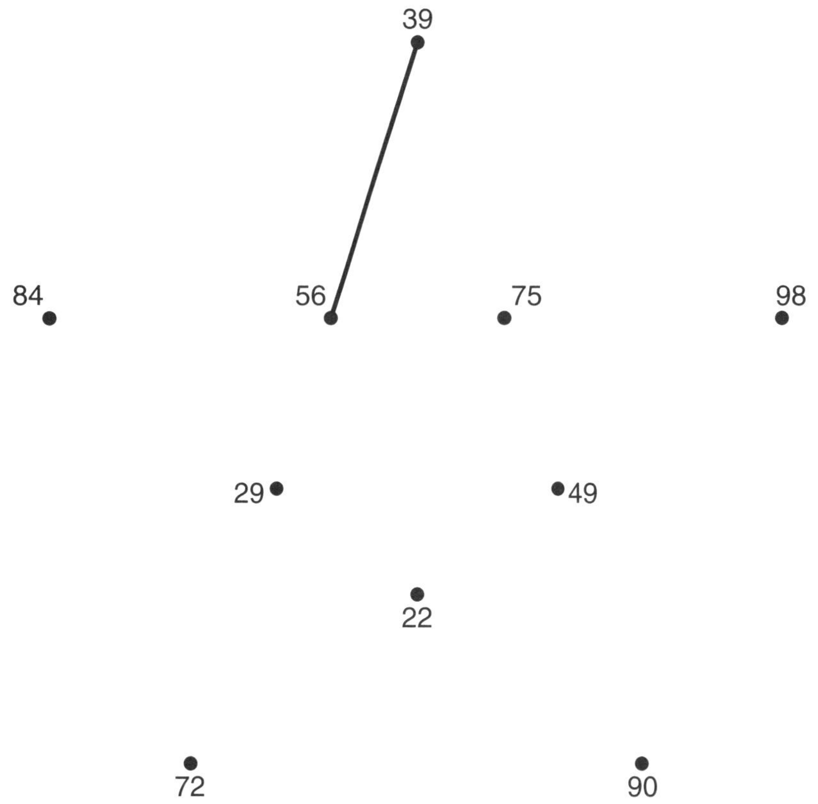

10
$$35 + 21$$

39

84   56   75   98

29   49

22

72   90

Regroup and Add

Solve the problems by regrouping.

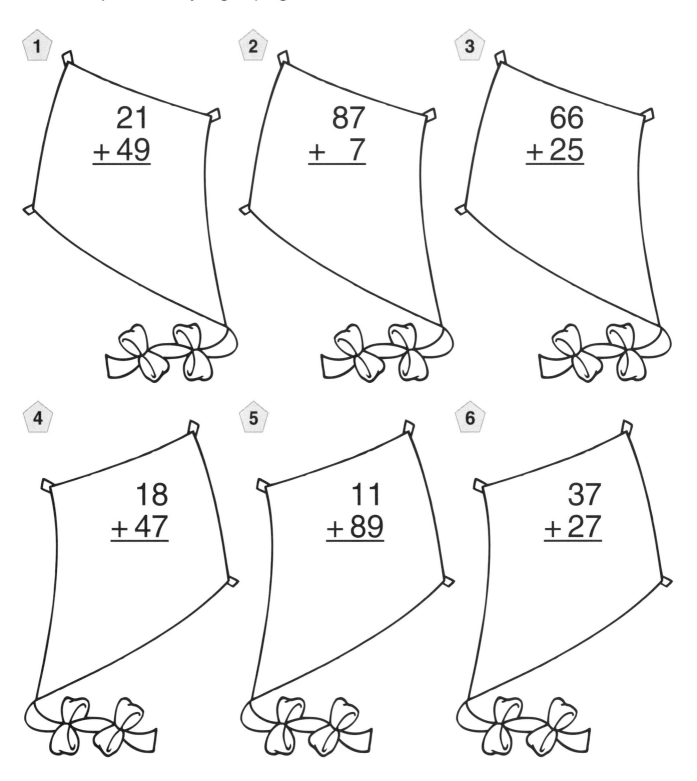

1.
$$21$$
$$+49$$

2.
$$87$$
$$+\ 7$$

3.
$$66$$
$$+25$$

4.
$$18$$
$$+47$$

5.
$$11$$
$$+89$$

6.
$$37$$
$$+27$$

Color the kites with *even* sums blue. Color the kites with *odd* sums red.

Regroup and Add

Find the sums on each notepad.

1
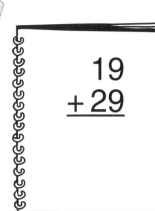
$$19$$
$$+29$$

2

$$15$$
$$+15$$

3
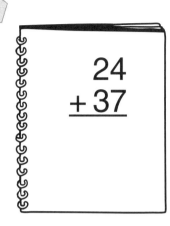
$$24$$
$$+37$$

4
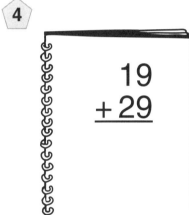
$$19$$
$$+29$$

5

$$19$$
$$+\ \ 8$$

6
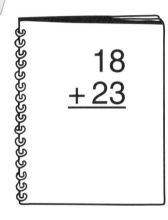
$$18$$
$$+23$$

7
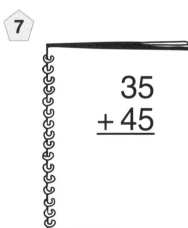
$$35$$
$$+45$$

8
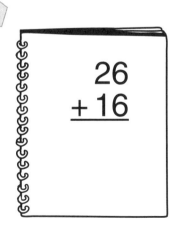
$$26$$
$$+16$$

9
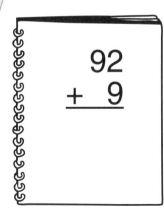
$$92$$
$$+\ \ 9$$

Color the notepads with sums greater than 40 red. Color the notepads with sums less than 40 purple.

Find each sum.

1

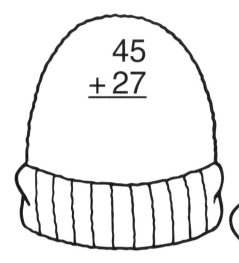

45
+27

2

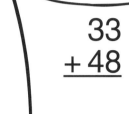

33
+48

3

16
+25

4

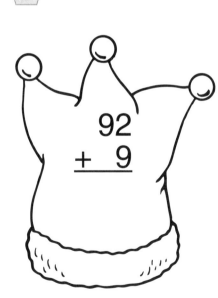

92
+ 9

5

53
+37

6

18
+13

7 Arrange the sums in order from *least* to *greatest*.

_____, _____, _____, _____, _____, _____

Regroup and Add

Solve the problems to help the frogs find their lily pads. Draw a line from each frog to its lily pad.

100   **105**   **114**   **93**   **143**   **125**

1

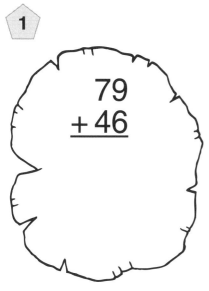

79
+46

2

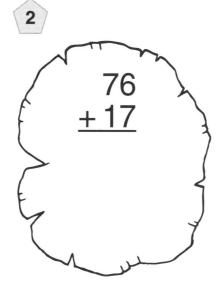

76
+17

3

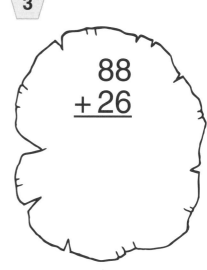

88
+26

4

69
+31

5

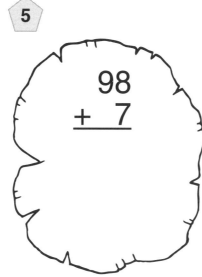

98
+ 7

6

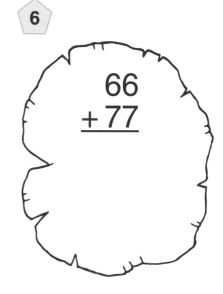

66
+77

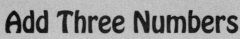

1	2	3
39 57 +47	33 75 +23	17 21 +53

4	5	6
42 26 +29	68 62 +56	61 33 +63

7	8	9
39 72 +12	151 24 + 81	42 84 +19

1

```
  96
  57
+ 67
```

2

```
  73
  74
+ 33
```

3

```
  56
  29
+ 55
```

4

```
  52
  30
+ 18
```

5

```
  17
  79
+ 54
```

6

```
  27
  77
+ 70
```

7

```
  59
  44
+ 16
```

8

```
  51
  24
+ 36
```

9

```
  67
  73
+ 30
```

Regroup and Add 3-Digit Numbers

Solve the problems. Use the code at the bottom to color each balloon.

1

149
+ 239

2

427
+ 518

3

218
+ 118

4

538
+ 258

5

616
+ 336

6

447
+ 216

7

827
+ 27

8

427
+ 118

854 = yellow	952 = green	388 = orange	663 = purple
945 = blue	545 = pink	336 = red	796 = brown

©Teacher Created Resources

Regroup and Add 3-Digit Numbers

Solve the problems. Good luck.

  1

$$236 \atop + 17$$

  2

$$456 \atop + 316$$

3

$$947 \atop + 38$$

4

$$222 \atop + 119$$

  5

$$515 \atop + 49$$

6

$$277 \atop + 39$$

7

$$125 \atop + 77$$

8

$$224 \atop + 648$$

  9

$$254 \atop + 216$$

10

$$637 \atop + 48$$

11

$$781 \atop + 19$$

12

$$446 \atop + 346$$

Addition Word Problems

Yesterday the second graders practiced jumping. Today the students recorded their best jumps.

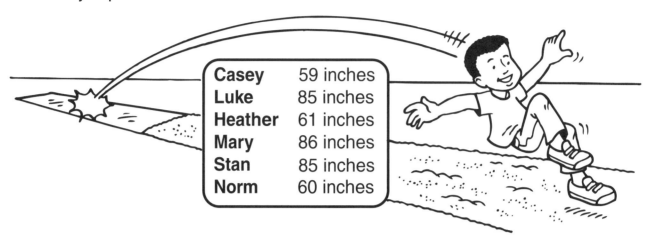

Casey	59 inches
Luke	85 inches
Heather	61 inches
Mary	86 inches
Stan	85 inches
Norm	60 inches

1 How far did Heather and Casey jump?

$$61$$
$$+\ 59$$ _____ inches

4 How far did Casey and Mary jump?

$$+$$ _____ inches

2 How far did Norm and Stan jump?

$$+$$ _____ inches

5 Who jumped the farthest?

_____

3 How far did Stan and Mary jump?

$$+$$ _____ inches

6 Which two jumpers jumped the same distance?

_____

and

_____

Addition Word Problems

Last week, Ralph and James kept a record of the pages they read each day. Here are their totals:

Ralph
Monday 20
Tuesday 29
Wednesday 25
Thursday 23
Friday 16

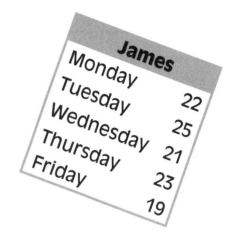

James
Monday 22
Tuesday 25
Wednesday 21
Thursday 23
Friday 19

Use the record of each boy's reading for the week to answer the questions below.

1. How many pages did they read on Monday? _____

2. How many pages did they read on Wednesday? _____

3. How many pages did they read on Friday? _____

4. Tuesday was the day each boy read the most. How many pages did they read that day? _____

5. Which day did they read the least? _____

6. How many pages did Ralph read all together? _____

7. How many pages did James read all together? _____

8. Who read more pages? _____

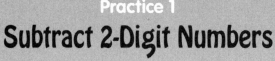

Subtract 2-Digit Numbers

There are four more subtraction problems and answers hidden in the number squares below. Three problems go across and one goes down. None of the problems are arranged diagonally. Find and circle the problems.

12 – 8 = 4			11
23	7	16	3
80	55	25	8
6	19	17	2

Write the problems you found above on the lines below.

_____ – _____ = _____

_____ – _____ = _____

_____ – _____ = _____

_____ – _____ = _____

Subtract 2-Digit Numbers

Solve each subtraction problem. Color the space blue if the difference is greater than (**>**) 10. Color the space orange if the difference is less than (**<**) 10.

1	2	3
$\begin{array}{r} 15 \\ -\ \ 0 \\ \hline \end{array}$	$\begin{array}{r} 21 \\ -10 \\ \hline \end{array}$	$\begin{array}{r} 45 \\ -30 \\ \hline \end{array}$

4	5	6
$\begin{array}{r} 63 \\ -42 \\ \hline \end{array}$	$\begin{array}{r} 25 \\ -24 \\ \hline \end{array}$	$\begin{array}{r} 37 \\ -30 \\ \hline \end{array}$

7	8	9
$\begin{array}{r} 28 \\ -26 \\ \hline \end{array}$	$\begin{array}{r} 45 \\ -41 \\ \hline \end{array}$	$\begin{array}{r} 18 \\ -13 \\ \hline \end{array}$

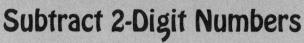

Solve the subtraction problems. Use the Color Code to color each ribbon.

1

$$81 - 3$$

2

$$78 - 4$$

3

$$65 - 6$$

4

$$35 - 7$$

5

$$53 - 2$$

6

$$37 - 8$$

7

$$97 - 8$$

Color Code

28 = red	59 = blue
29 = purple	78 = orange
51 = pink	89 = yellow
74 = green	

Solve each subtraction problem. Find out which player scored the winning goal.

1

GARCIA

```
  72
- 59
```

2

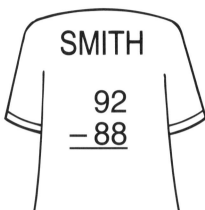

SMITH

```
  92
- 88
```

3

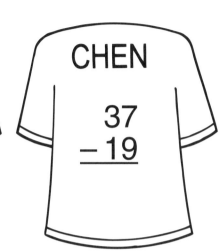

CHEN

```
  37
- 19
```

4

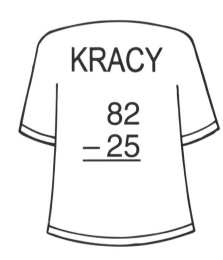

KRACY

```
  82
- 25
```

5

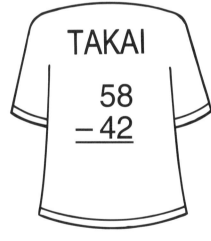

TAKAI

```
  58
- 42
```

6

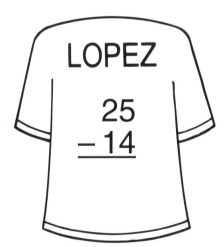

LOPEZ

```
  25
- 14
```

7 The player with a 6 on his jersey scored the goal. Which player was it?

Player: _____

Subtract 2-Digit Numbers

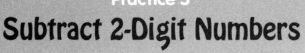

Play **Tic-Tac-Subtract** with 2-digit numbers. Solve each subtraction problem. To win, draw a line through the three boxes that have *sevens* in their differences.

1 $\begin{array}{r} 66 \\ -39 \\ \hline \end{array}$	**2** $\begin{array}{r} 97 \\ -28 \\ \hline \end{array}$	**3** $\begin{array}{r} 37 \\ -19 \\ \hline \end{array}$
4 $\begin{array}{r} 58 \\ -19 \\ \hline \end{array}$	**5** $\begin{array}{r} 85 \\ -68 \\ \hline \end{array}$	**6** $\begin{array}{r} 73 \\ -18 \\ \hline \end{array}$
7 $\begin{array}{r} 72 \\ -19 \\ \hline \end{array}$	**8** $\begin{array}{r} 39 \\ -16 \\ \hline \end{array}$	**9** $\begin{array}{r} 93 \\ -18 \\ \hline \end{array}$

Subtract 3-Digit Numbers

Complete the subtraction problems below.

1	**2**
$\begin{array}{r} 152 \\ -\ \ 71 \\ \hline \end{array}$	$\begin{array}{r} 188 \\ -\ \ 94 \\ \hline \end{array}$
3	**4**
$\begin{array}{r} 134 \\ -\ \ 42 \\ \hline \end{array}$	$\begin{array}{r} 136 \\ -\ \ 75 \\ \hline \end{array}$
5	**6**
$\begin{array}{r} 169 \\ -\ \ 87 \\ \hline \end{array}$	$\begin{array}{r} 207 \\ -\ \ 56 \\ \hline \end{array}$

Subtract 3-Digit Numbers

Play **Tic-Tac-Subtract** with 3-digit numbers. Solve each subtraction problem. To win, draw a line through the three spaces that have *ones* in their differences.

1

$$288 - 31$$

2

$$198 - 77$$

3

$$259 - 36$$

4

$$326 - 26$$

5

$$567 - 36$$

6

$$455 - 51$$

7

$$555 - 33$$

8

$$897 - 76$$

9

$$654 - 51$$

Regroup and Subtract 3-Digit Numbers

Find the difference for each subtraction problem. Use the answers to fill in the puzzle. Some numbers will be placed across (horizontal) and some will be placed down (vertical).

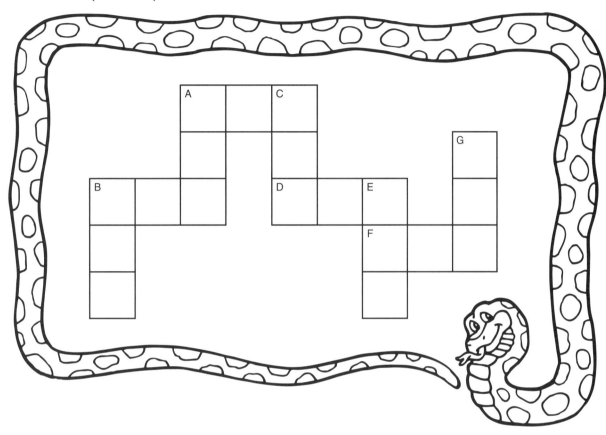

Across

A	B	D	F
501 − 114	908 − 723	601 − 9	907 − 35

Down

A	B	C	E	G
509 − 164	505 − 320	802 − 77	602 − 317	601 − 279

Regroup and Subtract 3-Digit Numbers

Find the difference in each subtraction problem.

1

$$543$$
$$- 295$$

2

$$661$$
$$- 573$$

3

$$427$$
$$- 338$$

4

$$609$$
$$- 129$$

5

$$724$$
$$- 639$$

6

$$712$$
$$- 633$$

7

$$944$$
$$- 726$$

8

$$856$$
$$- 49$$

9 One problem does not have an 8 in the answer. What shape is that problem in? Circle the correct shape word.

    oval   rectangle   square   triangle   octagon

Regroup and Subtract 3-Digit Numbers

Complete each subtraction problem. Use the answers to solve the riddle below.

a
$$932 - 236$$

e
$$676 - 591$$

t
$$991 - 309$$

f
$$179 - 80$$

i
$$817 - 281$$

r
$$519 - 370$$

What kind of tree is warm in the winter?

696	99	536	149	682	149	85	85
____	____	____	____	____	____	____	____

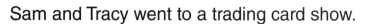

Sam and Tracy went to a trading card show.

1 Tracy had 58 trading cards. She dropped them in the parking lot and 22 blew away. How many cards did she have left?

_____

2 Sam had 143 trading cards and he gave 50 to Tracy. How many cards does Sam have left?

_____

3 Who has more cards now, Sam or Tracy?

_____

Three dogs were at the dog show. Zippy weighed 29 pounds. Monster weighed 62 pounds, and Goliath weighed 95 pounds.

4 How much more did Goliath weigh than Zippy? _____ pounds

5 How much more did Monster weigh than Zippy? _____ pounds

6 What is the difference in weight between Goliath and Monster?

_____

Subtraction Word Problems

There are many different kinds of shoes at the store. Each shoe has a different price. Use the display to solve the subtraction problems below. Show your work.

1	How much more does a pair of running shoes cost than a pair of cleats?	

2	What is the difference in cost between the running shoes and the dress shoes?	

3	What is the difference between the cowboy boots and the cleats?	

4	What is the difference between the price of the most expensive shoes and the price of the least expensive shoes?	

Repeat Addition–2s

1 Fill in the missing numbers in the grid.

1		3		5		7		9	
11		13		15		17		19	
21		23		25		27		29	
31		33		35		37		39	
41		43		45		47		49	
51		53		55		57		59	
61		63		65		67		69	
71		73		75		77		79	
81		83		85		87		89	
91		93		95		97		99	

2 Are the numbers you filled in even or odd? _____

3 Count forward by twos.

32	34		38		42	44		48

20	22		26		30			36

4 Count backward by twos.

80	78			72		68		64

1 Can you count by twos? Fill in the blanks below and see. All the numbers will be **even** numbers.

2, 4, _____, 8, _____, 12, 14, _____, 18, 20,

22, _____, 26, _____, 30, _____, 34, 36, 38, _____,

42, _____, _____, 48, 50, 52, _____, 56, _____, 60

Write the number that comes **two before** and **two after** each number below.

2 _____ 68 _____

3 _____ 72 _____

4 _____ 42 _____

5 _____ 76 _____

6 _____ 80 _____

7 _____ 88 _____

8 _____ 94 _____

9 _____ 98 _____

10 Color the pairs of socks below that have **even** numbers in them.

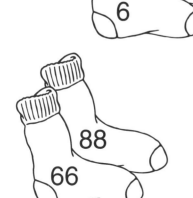

The groups or sets of marbles are arranged in groups of two. These *pairs* can be added or multiplied to find the sum.

 = __6__

2 + 2 + 2 = 6
or
2 x 3 = 6

Find the total number of marbles in each row by adding. Then write the information as a multiplication equation in the column on the right.

1

_____ + _____ = _____   _____ x _____ = _____

2

_____ + _____ + _____ + _____ = _____   _____ x _____ = _____

3

_____ + _____ + _____ = _____   _____ x _____ = _____

4

_____ + _____ + _____ + _____ + _____ = _____   _____ x _____ = _____

Rewrite each addition problem as a multiplication problem.

| **1** | There were two mini hamburgers for each boy. There were six boys. How many hamburgers were there? |

_____ × _____ = _____

| **2** | Mrs. Smith received two letters every day for three days. How many letters did she receive? |

_____ × _____ = _____

| **3** | There were four pairs of tennis shoes on the deck last night. How many shoes were on the deck? |

_____ × _____ = _____

| **4** | There are two socks to a pair. There are eight pairs of socks. How many socks are there? |

_____ × _____ = _____

Practice your 2s multiplication facts.

1 $2 \times 1 = \underline{\hspace{2cm}}$	**6** $2 \times 6 = \underline{\hspace{2cm}}$
2 $2 \times 2 = \underline{\hspace{2cm}}$	**7** $2 \times 7 = \underline{\hspace{2cm}}$
3 $2 \times 3 = \underline{\hspace{2cm}}$	**8** $2 \times 8 = \underline{\hspace{2cm}}$
4 $2 \times 4 = \underline{\hspace{2cm}}$	**9** $2 \times 9 = \underline{\hspace{2cm}}$
5 $2 \times 5 = \underline{\hspace{2cm}}$	**10** $2 \times 10 = \underline{\hspace{2cm}}$

11 Write a multiplication sentence for the swans below.

$\underline{\hspace{2cm}}$ x $\underline{\hspace{2cm}}$ = $\underline{\hspace{2cm}}$

12 Write a multiplication sentence for the birds below.

$\underline{\hspace{2cm}}$ x $\underline{\hspace{2cm}}$ = $\underline{\hspace{2cm}}$

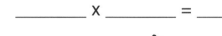

Repeat Addition–3s

Count by threes. Fill in the missing numbers in each row.

1 3   6   _____   12   15   _____   21   _____   27

2 30   33   _____   39   _____   45   _____   51

3 57   _____   63   _____   _____   72   75

4 81   _____   87   90   _____   96   _____

5 Circle the *odd* numbers.

6 Are all the numbers circled?   **YES**   **NO**

Count backwards by threes.

7 21   _____   _____   _____   _____   _____   _____

8 45   _____   _____   _____   _____   _____   _____

---

9 There are three marbles in each bag. How many marbles are there all together?

_____ + _____ + _____ + _____ = _____

---

10 There are three marbles in each bag. How many marbles are there all together?

_____ + _____ + _____ + _____ + _____ = _____

---

1 Can you count by threes? Fill in the blanks below and see.

3, 6, _____, 12, _____, _____, 21, 24, _____,

30, 33, _____, 39, _____, 45, _____ 51, _____,

57, _____, 63, _____, _____, 72, 75, _____,

81, _____, 87, 90, _____, 96, _____

2 Circle the numbers above that are *even* numbers.

Write the number that comes three *before* and three *after* each number below.

3 _____ 63 _____	7 _____ 84 _____
4 _____ 72 _____	8 _____ 51 _____
5 _____ 43 _____	9 _____ 92 _____
6 _____ 30 _____	10 _____ 97 _____

Look at the aliens below! Each alien has three eyes. Count the eyes on each alien to find out the total number of eyes in each row.

11		3 x 2 = _____ eyes
12		3 x 4 = _____ eyes
13		3 x 3 = _____ eyes
14		3 x 5 = _____ eyes

Multiply 3s

Adding groups of three is the same as multiplying groups of three. First find the total number of circles in each row by adding the groups. Solve the multiplication equation for the same groups of circles in the column on the right.

1

_____ + _____ + _____ + _____ + _____ + _____ = 18   3 x 6 = _____

2

_____ + _____ + _____ + _____ = _____   3 x 4 = _____

3

_____ + _____ + _____ + _____ + _____ + _____ + _____ = _____   3 x 7 = _____

4

_____ + _____ + _____ + _____ + _____ = _____   3 x 5 = _____

5 Draw three triangles, three squares, and three rhombi.

6

How many shapes did you draw in box 5? _____

7 Write and solve the problem as an addition problem.

_____ + _____ + _____ = _____

8 Write and solve the problem as a multiplication problem.

_____ x _____ = _____

Multiply by three to find out how many shapes are in each box.

1

3 × _____ = _____

2

3 × _____ = _____

3

3 × _____ = _____

4

3 × _____ = _____

5 Mr. Todd is planning an art project. He put three paintbrushes in each can.
How many paintbrushes are there in all?

_____ × _____ = _____

Practice your 3s multiplication facts.

1 3 × 1 = _____	**6** 3 × 6 = _____
2 3 × 2 = _____	**7** 3 × 7 = _____
3 3 × 3 = _____	**8** 3 × 8 = _____
4 3 × 4 = _____	**9** 3 × 9 = _____
5 3 × 5 = _____	**10** 3 × 10 = _____

11 | Write a multiplication sentence for the shells below.

_____ x _____ = _____

12 | Write a multiplication sentence for the seahorses below.

_____ x _____ = _____

Repeat Addition–5s

Can you count by **5s** to one hundred? Fill in the hands below and see.

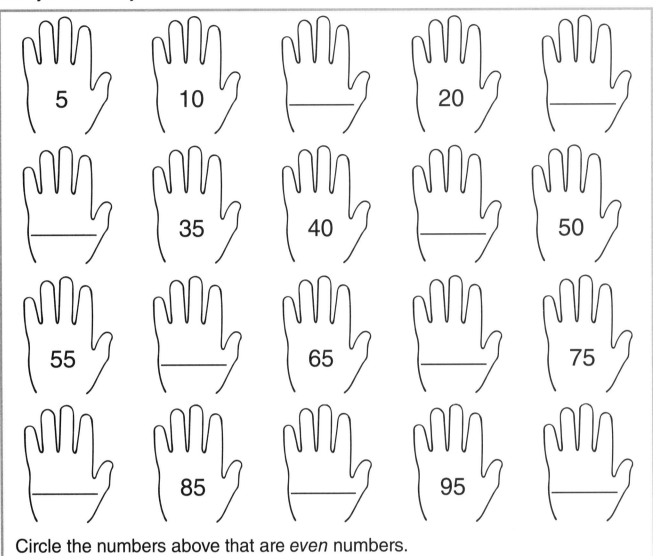

5	10	___	20	___
___	35	40	___	50
55	___	65	___	75
___	85	___	95	___

Circle the numbers above that are *even* numbers.

Write the number that comes five *before* and five *after* each number below.

1 ____ 20 ____	2 ____ 35 ____
3 ____ 85 ____	4 ____ 55 ____
5 ____ 10 ____	6 ____ 90 ____
7 ____ 45 ____	8 ____ 75 ____
9 ____ 60 ____	10 ____ 15 ____

Repeat Addition–5s

Look at the groups of happy faces in each row. There are five happy faces in each group. Add the groups to find out how many faces are in each row.

1

_____ + _____ + _____ = _____

2

_____ + _____ + _____ + _____ = _____

3

_____ + _____ + _____ + _____ + _____ + _____ = _____

4

_____ + _____ + _____ + _____ + _____ + _____ + _____ = _____

5

_____ + _____ + _____ + _____ + _____ = _____

Multiply 5s

Adding by groups of five is the same as multiplying groups of 5. Circle each group of five items in the box below. Find out how many groups of 5 are in the box.

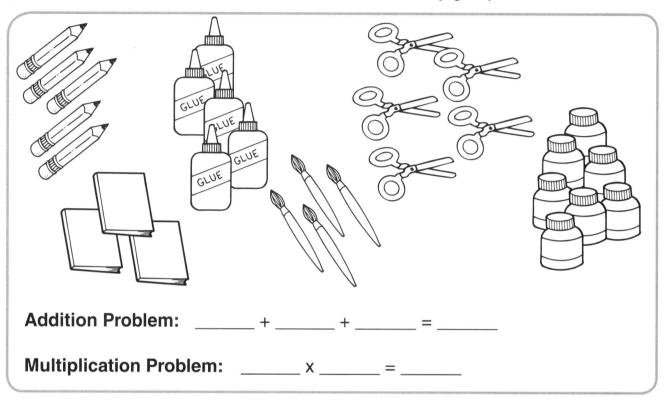

Addition Problem: _____ + _____ + _____ = _____

Multiplication Problem: _____ x _____ = _____

Look at the sets of shapes below. Add more shapes to each box to make each group a set of five.

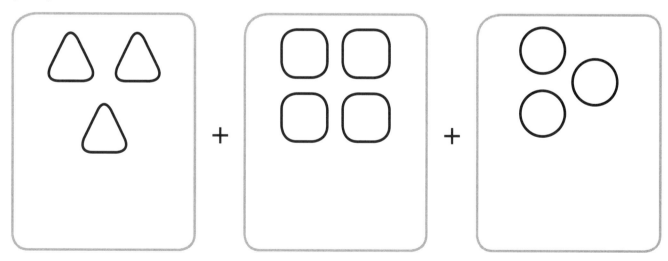

1. Write and solve the problem as an addition problem. _____

2. Write and solve the problem as a multiplication problem. _____

3. How many shapes do you have all together? _____

Adding groups of five is the same as multiplying groups of five. Find the total number of marbles in each row by adding. Then complete each multiplication equation in the column on the right.

1 ⬭⬭⬭⬭⬭ ⬭⬭⬭⬭⬭ 5 + 5 = _____	5 x 2 = _____
2 (four groups of 5 marbles) 5 + 5 + 5 + 5 = _____	5 x 4 = _____
3 (three groups of 5 marbles) 5 + 5 + 5 = _____	5 x 3 = _____
4 (five groups of 5 marbles) 5 + 5 + 5 + 5 + 5 = _____	5 x 5 = _____

Multiply by five to find out how many shapes are in each box below.

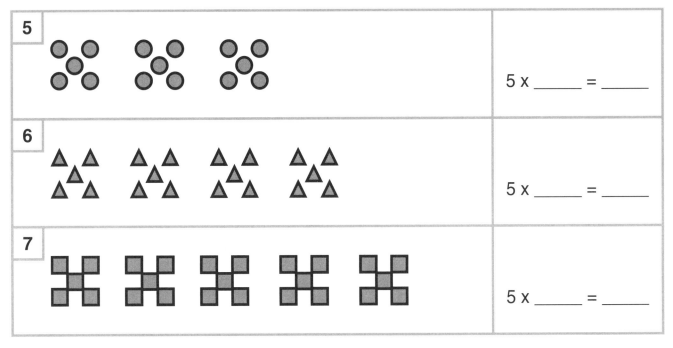

5 (three groups of 5 circles)	5 x _____ = _____
6 (four groups of 5 triangles)	5 x _____ = _____
7 (five groups of 5 squares)	5 x _____ = _____

Practice your 5s multiplication facts.

1 $5 \times 1 =$ _____	**6** $5 \times 6 =$ _____
2 $5 \times 2 =$ _____	**7** $5 \times 7 =$ _____
3 $5 \times 3 =$ _____	**8** $5 \times 8 =$ _____
4 $5 \times 4 =$ _____	**9** $5 \times 9 =$ _____
5 $5 \times 5 =$ _____	**10** $5 \times 10 =$ _____

Multiply by 5. Circle the correct answer in each row.

11 $5 \times 6 =$	30	25	40	65
12 $5 \times 9 =$	10	60	95	45
13 $5 \times 2 =$	5	10	25	50
14 $5 \times 7 =$	40	35	60	75
15 $5 \times 5 =$	35	45	55	25
16 $5 \times 8 =$	80	40	50	85
17 $5 \times 4 =$	10	15	20	45
18 $5 \times 0 =$	5	0	50	55

Repeat Addition–10s

---

1 Count by 10s to 100.

10, _____, _____, _____, _____, _____, _____, _____, _____, _____

Write the number that comes ten *before* and ten *after* the numbers below.

2 _____ 20 _____   **7** _____ 33 _____

3 _____ 85 _____   **8** _____ 58 _____

4 _____ 10 _____   **9** _____ 90 _____

5 _____ 47 _____   **10** _____ 74 _____

6 _____ 60 _____   **11** _____ 12 _____

There are ten balloons in every bunch. Count by tens to see how many balloons there are in each group.

12

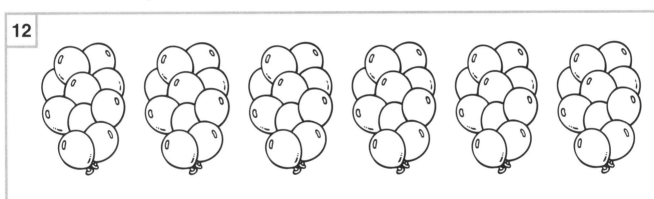

_____ + _____ + _____ + _____ + _____ + _____ = _____

13

_____ + _____ + _____ + _____ + _____ + _____ + _____ + _____ = _____

Each domino has ten dots. How many dots are in each problem?

1

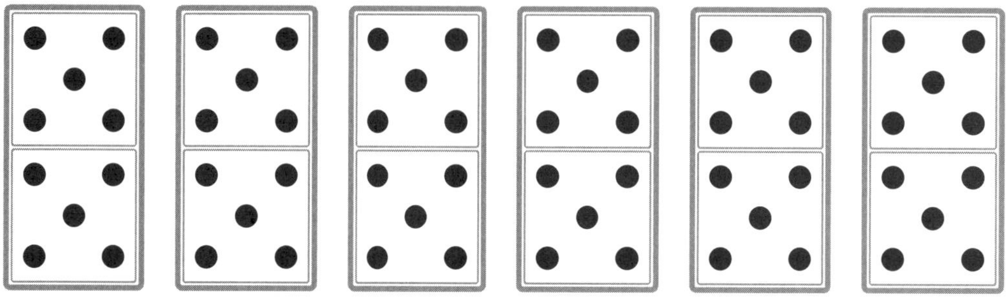

_____ + _____ + _____ + _____ + _____ + _____ = _____

2

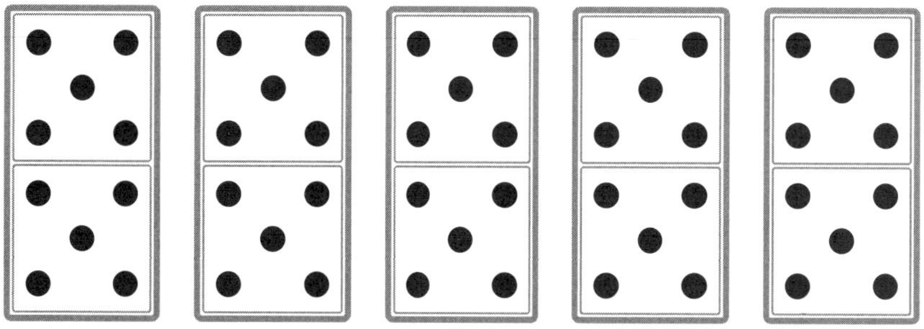

_____ + _____ + _____ + _____ + _____ = _____

Write the number that comes 10 *before* and 10 *after* each number below.

3 _____ 36 _____

7 _____ 58 _____

4 _____ 27 _____

8 _____ 15 _____

5 _____ 83 _____

9 _____ 49 _____

6 _____ 44 _____

10 _____ 79 _____

Multiply 10s

Adding groups of ten is the same as multiplying groups of ten. Find the total number of bugs in each box by adding. Then write the information as a multiplication equation.

1

10 + 10 + 10 = _____   10 x 3 = _____

2

10 + 10 + 10 + 10= _____   10 x 4 = _____

3

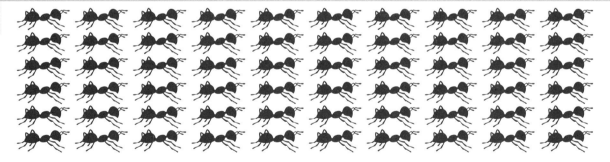

10 + 10 + 10 + 10 + 10 + 10 = _____   10 x 6 = _____

4   Callie has 10 snails and Joe has 10 snails. Mary has 10 snails and Jack has 10 snails. How many snails do they have in all?

Multiply 10s

Count by tens to fill in the missing numbers on the number lines below.

1

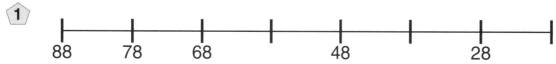

88   78   68   48   28

2

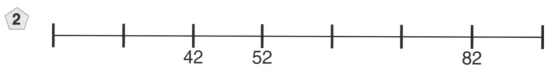

42   52   82

3

74   44   14

4

16   46   76

5

89   69   39

Count by tens to fill in the ladders below.

6

| 73 |
| 63 |
| |
| 43 |
| 33 |
| |

7

| |
| 55 |
| 65 |
| |
| |
| 95 |

8

| 11 |
| |
| |
| 41 |
| |
| 61 |

9

| 87 |
| |
| |
| 57 |
| |
| |

Multiply 10s

Practice your 10s multiplication facts.

1. $10 \times 1 =$ _____

2. $10 \times 2 =$ _____

3. $10 \times 3 =$ _____

4. $10 \times 4 =$ _____

5. $10 \times 5 =$ _____

6. $10 \times 6 =$ _____

7. $10 \times 7 =$ _____

8. $10 \times 8 =$ _____

9. $10 \times 9 =$ _____

10. $10 \times 10 =$ _____

Circle the correct answer in each row.

11 $10 \times 10 =$	20	10	40	100
12 $10 \times 4 =$	20	60	40	80
13 $10 \times 7 =$	70	80	90	60
14 $10 \times 5 =$	30	50	20	70
15 $10 \times 6 =$	20	50	60	90

Multiplication Word Problems

Solve the problems. Show your work.

---

1 Molly's mom dug three small holes in the garden. Molly put three seeds in each hole.

How many seeds did Molly plant in all?

_____ × _____ = _____

---

2 There are five bowls on the table. Jeff is filling each one with five oranges.

How many oranges will there be when Jeff is finished?

_____ × _____ = _____

---

3 There are ten pairs of socks in the basket.

How many socks are in the basket?

_____ × _____ = _____

---

4 There are three race cars at the starting line. Each race car has four huge wheels.

How many wheels are there at the starting line?

_____ × _____ = _____

Multiplication Word Problems

1 There are nine players on the team. Each player brought two bats to practice.

How many bats were there for practice? _____ × _____ = _____

2 There were five girls at the table. Each girl was wearing three rings.

How many rings were there? _____ × _____ = _____

3 Susan made a tally mark each day that it snowed in December.

┌─── **December Snow Days** ───┐
| ЖЖ   ЖЖ   ЖЖ   ЖЖ |
└──────────────────────────┘

How many days did it snow in December? _____ × _____ = _____

4 There are four chairs at the table. Each chair has four legs.

How many chair legs are there all together? _____ × _____ = _____

Fractions $\frac{1}{2}$, $\frac{1}{3}$, $\frac{1}{4}$

A *fraction* is a part of a whole. Look at the circles below. Count how many parts each one has been divided into. Write the total number of parts on the line next to each circle.

1 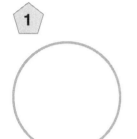 _____

2 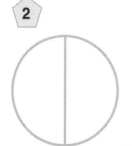 _____

3 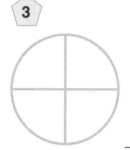 _____

Look at the shapes in each box below. Follow the directions below each group of shapes.

4 Draw a circle around the picture that shows the fraction $\frac{1}{2}$.

5 Draw a triangle on the picture that shows the fraction $\frac{1}{4}$.

6 Draw a rectangle on the picture that shows the fraction $\frac{1}{3}$.

7 Divide the square into four equal parts.

8 Divide the circle into two equal parts.

9 Divide the rectangle into three equal parts.

Fractions $\frac{1}{2}$, $\frac{1}{3}$, $\frac{1}{4}$

1

Color one half of the circle green. Color the other half of the circle yellow. How many halves make a whole? _____

2

What part of the hexagon is shaded? $\frac{1}{2}$ $\frac{1}{3}$ $\frac{1}{4}$

3

Color one third of the rectangle blue and one third of the rectangle red. Leave one third white. How many thirds make a whole? _____

4

What part of the rhombus is shaded? $\frac{1}{2}$ $\frac{1}{3}$ $\frac{1}{4}$

5

Color one quarter of the rectangle purple and one quarter pink. Color two quarters blue. How many quarters make a whole? _____

6

What part of the rectangle is shaded?
$\frac{1}{2}$ $\frac{1}{3}$ $\frac{1}{4}$

7

Color half the leaves. How many did you color? _____ out of _____

8

Color four flowers. How many did you color? $\frac{1}{2}$ $\frac{1}{3}$ $\frac{1}{4}$

Fractions $\frac{1}{2} - \frac{1}{6}$

Look at the rectangles on the left. Draw a line to match the shaded part of the shape with the fraction on the right.

 1

$\frac{1}{5}$

 2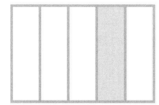

$\frac{1}{2}$

3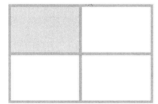

$\frac{1}{4}$

 4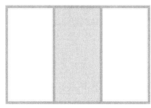

$\frac{1}{6}$

 5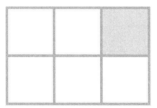

$\frac{1}{3}$

How many stars are circled? Fill in the blanks below each set of stars to complete each statement.

6 _____ out of _____   7 _____ out of _____   8 _____ out of _____

Fractions $\frac{1}{2} - \frac{1}{6}$

Look at the number of parts in each shape. How many parts in each shape are gray? Draw a line to the correct fraction. Remember, the top number is the *numerator* and the bottom number is the *denominator.*

1

$\frac{1}{2}$

2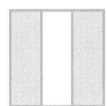

$\frac{2}{5}$

3

$\frac{2}{6}$

4

$\frac{3}{5}$

5

$\frac{2}{3}$

6

$\frac{1}{3}$

7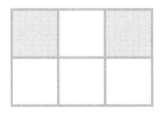

$\frac{3}{4}$

Fractions $\frac{1}{2} - \frac{1}{8}$

Color the correct number of parts of each shape to match the fraction under it. The first one has been done for you.

1

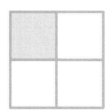

$\frac{1}{4}$

2

$\frac{2}{4}$

3

$\frac{1}{3}$

4

$\frac{2}{5}$

5

$\frac{4}{6}$

6

$\frac{2}{7}$

7

$\frac{3}{8}$

8

$\frac{1}{3}$

9

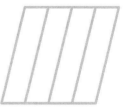

$\frac{3}{4}$

Fractions $\frac{1}{2} - \frac{1}{8}$

Color **some** fish in each bowl. Write a fraction for the amount of fish you colored.

Example: If you color 3 fish in a bowl with 4 fish, you would write $\frac{3}{4}$.

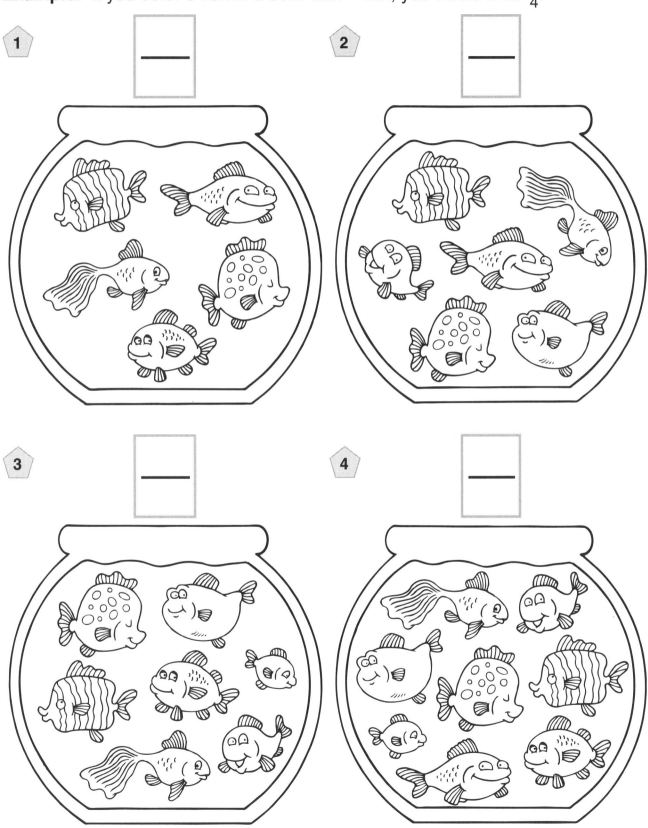

This birthday cake has two layers. It is divided into nine equal slices.

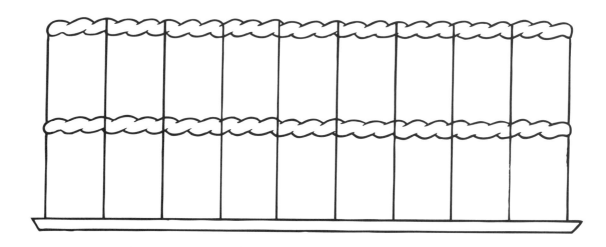

1 Dad ate three pieces. Color them red.

2 Mom ate two pieces. Color them blue.

3 Tommy ate one piece. Color it yellow.

4 How many pieces have not been eaten? _____ Write it as a fraction. _____

5 What fraction parts did mom and dad eat? _____ + _____ = _____

6 What fraction parts did Tommy and Dad eat? _____ + _____ = _____

The beach ball is divided into 10 equal sections.

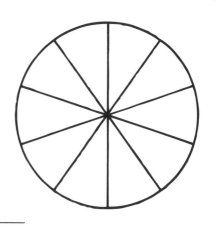

7 Color 3 parts green.

8 Color 2 sections purple.

9 What fractional part of the ball has not been colored? _____

10 What fractional part of the ball is green? _____

Fractions $\frac{1}{11} - \frac{1}{12}$

There are eleven birds at the feeder. Sarah wants to give each bird the same amount of bread so she cuts the bread into eleven pieces.

1 What fraction of the bread will three birds get?

_____

2 What fraction of the bread will five birds get?

_____

3 What fraction of the bread will seven birds get?

_____

4 Use a brown crayon to color the amount of bread 10 birds will get.

The sandwich for the soccer team was divided into 12 pieces. Color each player's portion a different color.

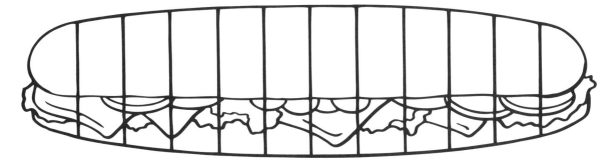

5 Brad ate two slices of the sandwich. What fraction did he eat? _____

6 Darin ate four slices of the sandwich. What fraction did he eat? _____

7 Steve ate five slices of the sandwich. What fraction did he eat? _____

8 How much was left for the coach? _____

Fraction Review $\frac{1}{2} - \frac{1}{12}$

Finish the fraction in each box. In some boxes the denominator has been given. Other boxes show the numerator.

Remember: The *denominator* shows how many items there are all together. The number of items circled in each group is the *numerator*.

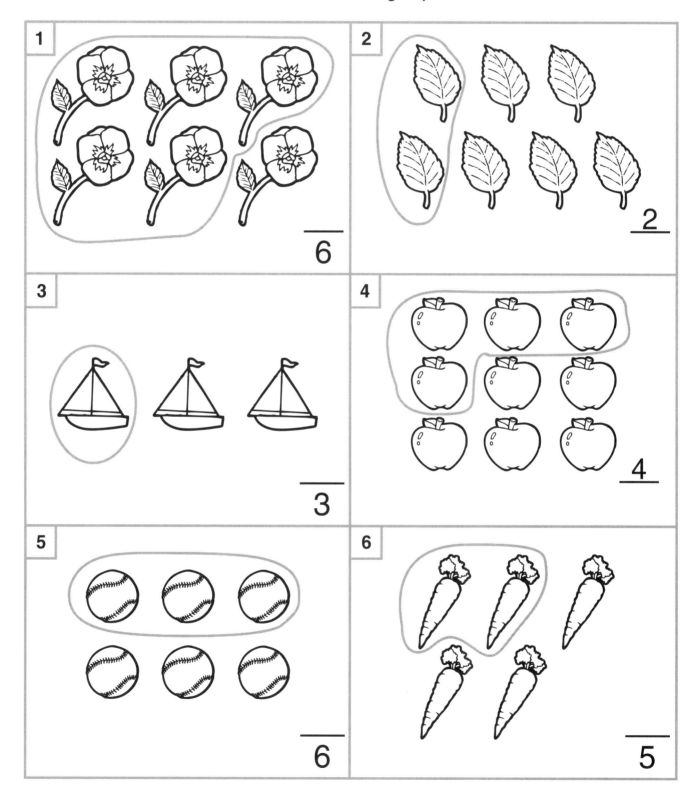

Fraction Review $\frac{1}{2} - \frac{1}{12}$

Look at the fraction in each small box. Circle the correct number of items in each large box to make the fraction true.

1

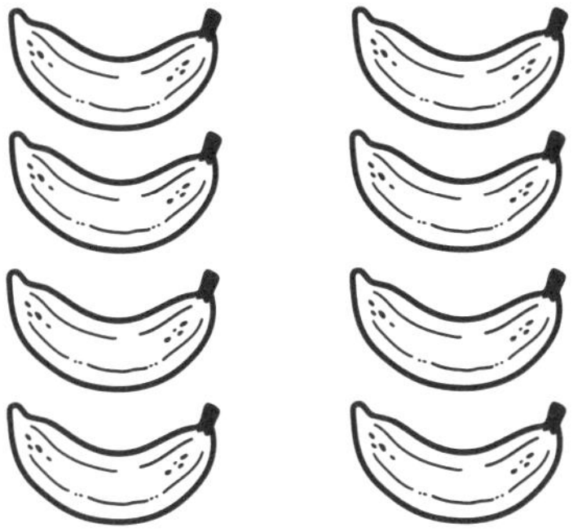

$\frac{3}{8}$

2

$\frac{5}{6}$

3

$\frac{7}{12}$

4

$\frac{2}{9}$

5

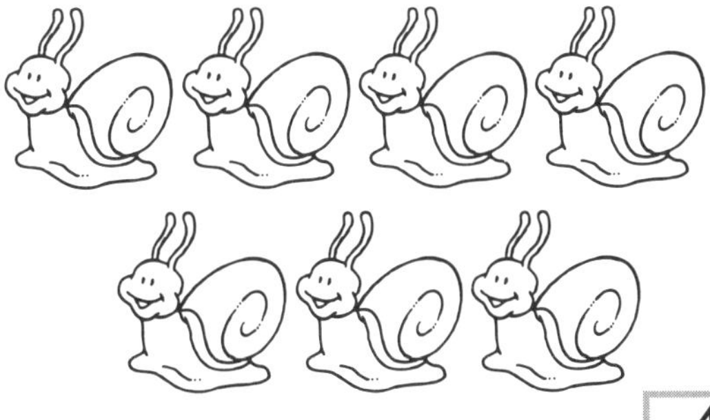

$\frac{4}{7}$

6

$\frac{3}{10}$

Read each word problem and circle, cross out, or fill in the art to help answer the questions.

1 Martha made a pie. She cut 10 slices. She served seven slices. How many slices are left?

_____

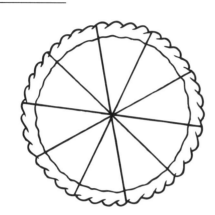

Show your answer as a fraction. _____

2 There were a dozen eggs on the tray. Five eggs rolled off the table and broke. How many eggs were left? _____

Show your answer as a fraction. _____

3 Axel had eight hamburgers. He gave half to his brother. How many hamburgers did he give his brother? _____ How many did he have left? _____

Circle the correct fraction to show how many hamburgers each boy got.

$$\frac{2}{8} \qquad \frac{4}{8} \qquad \frac{6}{8}$$

4 Nigel has seven dogs. He walked three in the morning and will walk the rest in the afternoon. How many dogs will he walk in the afternoon? _____

Circle the fraction to show how many dogs he will walk in the afternoon.

$$\frac{3}{7} \qquad \frac{4}{7} \qquad \frac{5}{7}$$

Fraction Word Problems

Solve the problems. Show your work.

1 Sammy had a whole apple pie. He cut it in half. How many pieces of pie did he have?

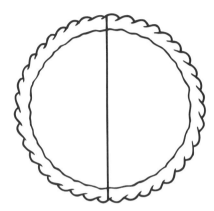

Sammy had _____ pieces of apple pie.

2 Rocky ordered a pizza. The pizza was cut into four equal slices. Rocky ate half the pizza. How many slices did Rocky eat?

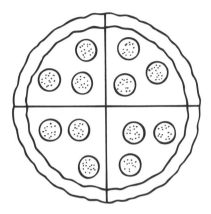

Rocky ate _____ slices of pizza.

3 Ralph had nine marbles. He kept one third of the marbles. He gave one third to Marcie and one third to Len. How many marbles did each person get?

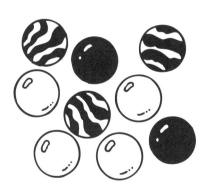

Each person got _____ marbles.

4 Marilyn had five apples. She gave away two fifths of the apples. How many apples did she have left?

Marilyn had _____ apples left.

Money–Coins

Every time Mrs. Smith does the laundry she finds coins in her son's pockets.

Draw a line from the list of coins on the left to the coins shown on the right.

1 **Monday**
2 quarters
1 dime
3 pennies

2 **Tuesday**
1 quarter
2 dimes
2 nickels
4 pennies

3 **Wednesday**
3 dimes
5 nickels
2 pennies

4 **Thursday**
2 quarters
3 nickels
1 penny

5 **Friday**
1 quarter
2 dimes
3 nickels
4 pennies

6 On what day did Mrs. Smith find the most money? _____

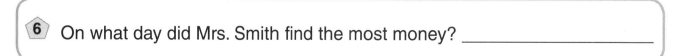

Sally planned to go to four movies during vacation. She planned the snacks she would buy for each movie, too. The movies and snacks are on the left. The coins used to pay are on the right. Draw a line to connect each trip to the movies with the correct list of coins spent.

1 Home Again

popcorn

soda

Total: $4.45

2 All I Want for Halloween

hot dog

soda

Total: $3.75

3 Sam the Fish

lemonade

popcorn

candy

Total: $5.00

4 Magic

soda

popcorn

Total: $3.05

20 quarters

16 quarters

4 dimes

5 pennies

10 quarters

4 dimes

3 nickels

35 dimes

5 nickels

Money–Dollars and Cents

The Wilson children each wanted to earn four dollars. Their parents posted eight jobs that could be done to earn the money. Fill in the chart below with the amount each child earned. Put a check in the last column if the child reached the goal.

Wash the windows. $2.00

Paint the fence. $3.00

Rake the leaves. $2.00

Walk the dog. 25¢

Wash the car. $3.00

Sort the recycling. $1.00

Pull the weeds. 75¢

Vacuum the car. $1.00

NAME	JOBS	TOTAL	REACHED GOAL
Annabelle	walked dog (2 times) sorted recycling washed windows vacuumed car		
Isabel	washed the car raked leaves		
Jordan	walked the dog (4 times) pulled weeds		
Logan	painted the fence pulled weeds walked the dog		

Who made the most money? _____

Money–Dollars and Cents

Find the total amount for each group of coins. Write the amount using a **cent sign(¢)**.

1 3 nickels and 7 pennies = _____

2 2 quarters, 1 dime, and 8 pennies = _____

3 2 quarters and 1 nickel = _____

4 4 dimes, 4 nickels, and 4 pennies = _____

5 4 dimes, 1 nickel, and three pennies = _____

In the grid below, shade the squares showing the totals from 1–5 above.

1	2	3	4	5	6	7	8	9	10
11	12	13	14	15	16	17	18	19	20
21	22	23	24	25	26	27	28	29	30
31	32	33	34	35	36	37	38	39	40
41	42	43	44	45	46	47	48	49	50
51	52	53	54	55	56	57	58	59	60
61	62	63	64	65	66	67	68	69	70
71	72	73	74	75	76	77	78	79	80
81	82	83	84	85	86	87	88	89	90
91	92	93	94	95	96	97	98	99	100

Find the total amount for each group of coins. Write the amount using a **dollar sign($)**.

6 2 quarters, 5 dimes, and 6 pennies = _____

7 1 quarter, 10 dimes, and 17 pennies = _____

8 2 quarters, 4 dimes, 1 nickel, and 5 pennies = _____

9 8 nickels and 65 pennies = _____

10 7 quarters and 7 pennies = _____

Money Word Problems

James wants a new soccer ball that costs $11.00. Each day he does jobs for his grandmother to earn the money. Solve each subtraction problem and finish the story. Does James get the new ball?

1 The soccer ball costs $11.00. On Monday James earned $4.00.

How many more dollars does he need to buy the ball?

_____ − _____ = _____

2 On Tuesday James earned $3.00. How much money has James earned?

_____ + _____ = _____

How many more dollars does he need to buy the ball?

_____ − _____ = _____

3 On Wednesday James earned $2.00. How much has James earned now?

_____ + _____ = _____

How many more dollars does he need to buy the ball?

_____ − _____ = _____

4 On Thursday James earned $3.00.

How much money has he earned?

_____ + _____ = _____

5 Can James buy a new soccer ball?

Yes   No

Money Word Problems

1 Lauren has 124 pennies. Her brother has 132 pennies. How many pennies do they have all together?

+ _____

Convert that amount to dollars and cents. $_____

2 David and Sonja each have $1.06 in coins. David has 12 coins and Sonja has 6 coins. Draw coins that each could have. Label each coin with its value as listed below. **Hint:** David and Sonja each have only one penny.

Dollar = $1.00

Fifty Cent = 50¢

Quarter = 25¢

Dime = 10¢

Nickel = 5¢

Penny = 1¢

David's Coins	Sonja's Coins

3 Three sisters went shopping for shoes. Jenny spent $15, Traci spent $22, and Naomi spent $18. What is the difference between the most expensive shoes and the least expensive shoes? How much did they spend all together?

Difference

_____ – _____ = _____

```
    22
    18
 +  15
_____
```

4 Silvia and Eddy each have twenty dollars in bills. Silvia has eight bills and Eddy has three bills. Show the amounts on the bills below.

Silvia

Eddy

Measurement–Longest, Shortest, Equal

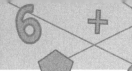

The items in each of the rows below are close in size. Follow the directions below for each row. Use a ruler if necessary.

1. Draw a rectangle around the longest item in each row.

2. Cross out the shortest item in each row.

3. Circle the two items that are equal in length in each row.

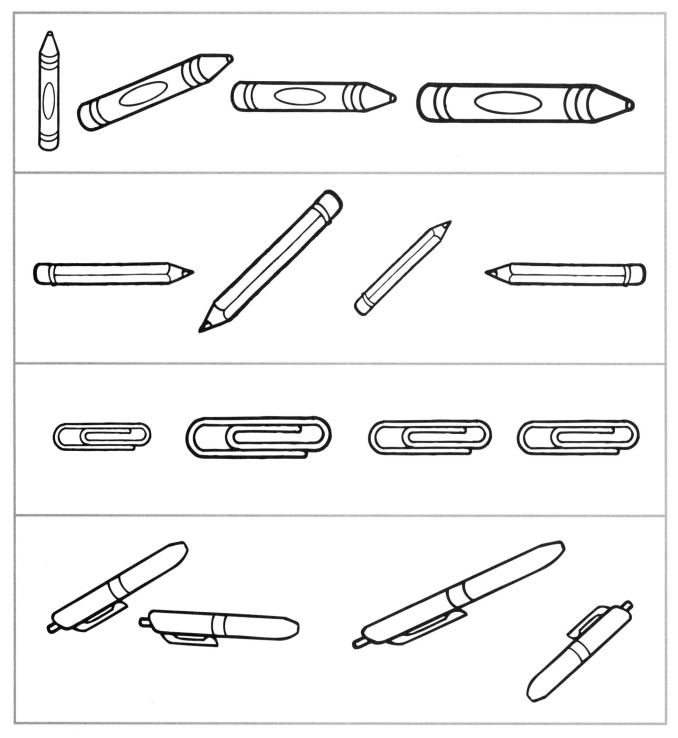

1 There are two trees in this picture.
Draw a tree that is taller than both trees.

Label the trees tall, taller, and tallest.

2 There are three scarves.
Circle the shortest scarf.

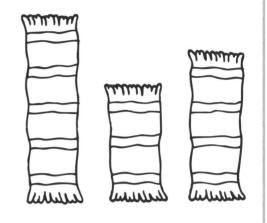

3 Draw a box that is equal in size to the box shown.

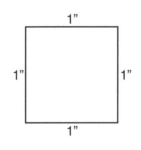

1"
1"   1"
1"

4 Circle the two pencils that are equal in size.

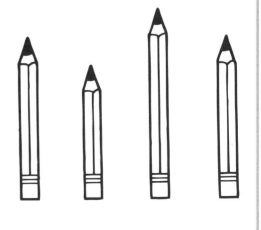

Measurement–Inches

Estimate how long each line is in inches. Write your estimate on the line. Use a ruler to measure each line. Write the correct measurement on the line next to the estimate. Were you close?

1 ————————————————————————————————

    Estimate _____   Measurement _____

2 ————————————————————

    Estimate _____   Measurement _____

3 ————————————————————————

    Estimate _____   Measurement _____

4 ——————————————————

    Estimate _____   Measurement _____

5 How long is the longest line? _____

6 How long is the shortest line? _____

7 If you combined Line 1 and Line 2 how long would it be? _____

8 The race car is 12 tires long. How many flags long is the car? _____

Measurement–Inches

Use a ruler to measure *height* and *width* in inches. Answer the questions below.

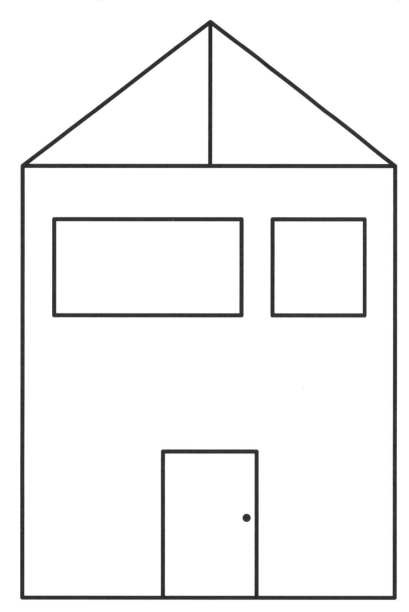

1 How wide is the house? _____

2 How tall is the house at its highest point? _____

3 What is the width of the door? _____

4 What is the height of the door? _____

5 What is the height of the square window? _____

6 What is the width of the window shaped like a rectangle? _____

7 What is the height of the window shaped like a rectangle? _____

Measurement–Centimeters

Use a ruler to measure each line in centimeters. Write the correct measurement on the line.

1 ├───┤

Measurement: _____ cm

2 ├──────────────────────────────────┤

Measurement: _____ cm

3 ├───────────────────────────────────────┤

Measurement: _____ cm

4 ├───────────────────────────────┤

Measurement: _____ cm

5 How long is the longest line? _____

6 How long is the shortest line? _____

7 If you combined Line 3 and Line 4 how long would it be?

_____ + _____ = _____

8 Measure the crayon box on the right. How many centimeters *wide* is it? _____

9 How many centimeters *tall* is the crayon box?

_____

Measurement–Feet

Plot how many feet each animal jumped and solve the problems.

| 2' | 4' | 3' | 8' |

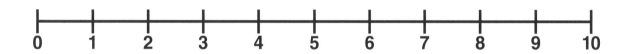

0   1   2   3   4   5   6   7   8   9   10

1 How much farther did the kangaroo jump than the horse?

_____ – _____ = _____ feet

2 How much farther did the kangaroo jump than the frog?

_____ – _____ = _____ feet

3 How much farther did the horse jump than the rabbit?

_____ – _____ = _____ foot

4 How much farther did the rabbit jump than the frog?

_____ – _____ = _____ foot

5 How much farther did the horse jump than the frog?

_____ – _____ = _____ feet

6 How much farther did the kangaroo jump than the rabbit?

_____ – _____ = _____ feet

Measurement–Miles

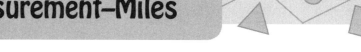

Plot how far each plane flew on the number line and solve the addition problems.

Plane 1   20 miles ⟶

Plane 2   30 miles ⟶

Plane 3   50 miles ⟶

Plane 4   70 miles ⟶

Plane 5   90 miles ⟶

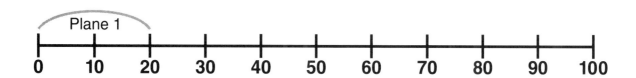

Plane 1

0   10   20   30   40   50   60   70   80   90   100

1 How far did Plane 1 and Plane 3 fly? _____ + _____ = _____

2 How far did Plane 2 and Plane 3 fly? _____ + _____ = _____

3 How far did Plane 4 and Plane 3 fly? _____ + _____ = _____

4 How far did Plane 2 and Plane 4 fly? _____ + _____ = _____

5 Which two planes flew a total of eighty miles? _____ and _____

6 Which three planes flew a total of one hundred miles? _____,
_____ and _____

Measurement–Pounds

Each pail of sand weighs 5 pounds. How many pounds of sand did each child collect?

1 Jack filled 4 pails.   _____ x _____ = _____

2 Jill filled 3 pails.   _____ x _____ = _____

3 Pete filled 2 pails.   _____ x _____ = _____

4 Lee filled 6 pails.   _____ x _____ = _____

5 If one pound is 16 ounces, how many ounces is two pounds?

_____ + _____ = _____ ounces   *or*   _____ x _____ = _____

---

6 Each basket of apples weighs two pounds. How much does each group of apples weigh?

_____ × _____ = _____ pounds

7

_____ × _____ = _____ pounds

8

_____ × _____ = _____ pounds

Measurement–Pounds

Five classmates went on a hayride at the farm. The old mule could only pull 200 pounds at a time. Use the weight chart to answer the questions below.

George	70 lbs.
Paul	80 lbs.
Darwin	65 lbs.
Elton	85 lbs.
Mick	60 lbs.

1 Which classmate weighs the least? _____

2 Who weights the most? _____

3 What is the difference between the heaviest and the lightest boy?

_____ – _____ = _____ pounds

4 Can the mule pull George, Mick, and Darwin at the same time? _____

Show your work:

5 Can the mule pull George, Paul, and Elton at the same time? _____

Show your work:

Measurement Word Problems

Solve each word problem. Show your work.

1. Denny's suitcase weighs 12 pounds and his mom's suitcase weighs 28 pounds. How much do their suitcases weigh together?

   _____ + _____ = _____ pounds

2. Is the total greater than 50 pounds or less than 50 pounds?

   _____

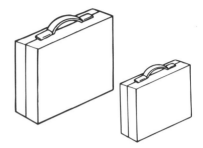

3. There is a pile of bricks in the yard. Each brick weighs two pounds. Starr moved 12 bricks. How many pounds of bricks did she move?

   _____ x _____ = _____ pounds

4. Is the total more than 20 pounds or less than 20 pounds?

   _____

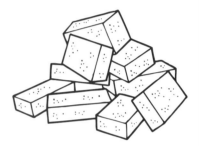

5. Mrs. Towne had five stacks of paper to recycle. Each stack weighs three pounds.

   Show your work:

   _____ x _____ = _____

   How many pounds of paper did

   Mrs. Towne have? _____ pounds

6. My backpack weighs seven pounds and my brother's backpack weighs 11 pounds. Our sister's backpack weighs four pounds.

   Show your work:

   How much do all three backpacks weigh? _____ pounds

Measurement Word Problems

Solve each word problem. Show your work.

Bike 1 weighs fourteen pounds.

Bike 2 weighs twenty-four pounds.

Bike 3 weighs thirty-three pounds.

1 Which bike weighs the least? _____

2 How much do Bike 1 and Bike 2 weigh together? _____

3 How much do Bike 2 and Bike 3 weigh together? _____

4 How much do the three bikes weigh all together? _____

Puppy 1 weighs four pounds.

Puppy 2 weighs eight pounds.

Puppy 3 weighs three pounds.

Puppy 4 weighs twelve pounds.

5 How much do the two heaviest puppies weigh together?

_____ + _____ = _____

6 How much do all four puppies weigh together?

_____ + _____ + _____ + _____ = _____

7 How much do the heaviest puppy and the lightest puppy weigh together?

_____ + _____ = _____

8 Which two puppies weigh as much as Puppy 4? _____ and _____

A Calendar Year

Look at the calendars for the year and answer the questions below.

1	How many days are in a week?	2	What month is your birthday month?
_____		_____	
3	How many months are in a year?	4	Which month comes before October?
_____		_____	
5	What is the last month of the year?	6	Which month comes after May?
_____		_____	
7	How many months have 31 days?	8	Which month has the fewest days?
_____		_____	

January

Sun	Mo	Tu	We	Th	Fr	Sa
1	2	3	4	5	6	7
8	9	10	11	12	13	14
15	16	17	18	19	20	21
22	23	24	25	26	27	28
29	30	31				

February

Sun	Mo	Tu	We	Th	Fr	Sa
			1	2	3	4
5	6	7	8	9	10	11
12	13	14	15	16	17	18
19	20	21	22	23	24	25
26	27	28				

March

Sun	Mo	Tu	We	Th	Fr	Sa
			1	2	3	4
5	6	7	8	9	10	11
12	13	14	15	16	17	18
19	20	21	22	23	24	25
26	27	28	29	30	31	

April

Sun	Mo	Tu	We	Th	Fr	Sa
						1
2	3	4	5	6	7	8
9	10	11	12	13	14	15
16	17	18	19	20	21	22
23	24	25	26	27	28	29
30						

May

Sun	Mo	Tu	We	Th	Fr	Sa
	1	2	3	4	5	6
7	8	9	10	11	12	13
14	15	16	17	18	19	20
21	22	23	24	25	26	27
28	29	30	31			

June

Sun	Mo	Tu	We	Th	Fr	Sa
				1	2	3
4	5	6	7	8	9	10
11	12	13	14	15	16	17
18	19	20	21	22	23	24
25	26	27	28	29	30	

July

Sun	Mo	Tu	We	Th	Fr	Sa
						1
2	3	4	5	6	7	8
9	10	11	12	13	14	15
16	17	18	19	20	21	22
23	24	25	26	27	28	29
30	31					

August

Sun	Mo	Tu	We	Th	Fr	Sa
		1	2	3	4	5
6	7	8	9	10	11	12
13	14	15	16	17	18	19
20	21	22	23	24	25	26
27	28	29	30	31		

September

Sun	Mo	Tu	We	Th	Fr	Sa
					1	2
3	4	5	6	7	8	9
10	11	12	13	14	15	16
17	18	19	20	21	22	23
24	25	26	27	28	29	30

October

Sun	Mo	Tu	We	Th	Fr	Sa
1	2	3	4	5	6	7
8	9	10	11	12	13	14
15	16	17	18	19	20	21
22	23	24	25	26	27	28
29	30	31				

November

Sun	Mo	Tu	We	Th	Fr	Sa
			1	2	3	4
5	6	7	8	9	10	11
12	13	14	15	16	17	18
19	20	21	22	23	24	25
26	27	28	29	30		

December

Sun	Mo	Tu	We	Th	Fr	Sa
					1	2
3	4	5	6	7	8	9
10	11	12	13	14	15	16
17	18	19	20	21	22	23
24	25	26	27	28	29	30
31						

August

Sunday	Monday	Tuesday	Wednesday	Thursday	Friday	Saturday
1	2	3	4	5	6	7
8	9	10	11	12	13	14
15	16	17	18	19	20	21
22	23	24	25	26	27	28
29	30	31				

1 Christopher's birthday is August 28. If today is August 1, how many days does he have to wait?

28 − 1 = _____

2 On August 6, how many more days will Christopher have to wait for his birthday?

_____ − _____ = _____

3 On August 19, how many more days will Christopher have to wait for his birthday?

_____ − _____ = _____

4 On August 24, how many more days will Christopher have to wait for his birthday?

_____ − _____ = _____

Write the time for each analog clock.

1	2	3
	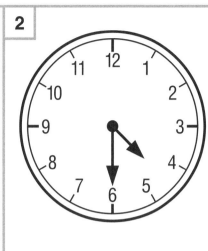	
_____ : _____	_____ : _____	_____ : _____

4	5	6
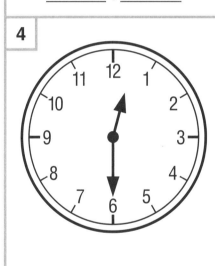		
_____ : _____	_____ : _____	_____ : _____

7	8	9

_____ : _____	_____ : _____	_____ : _____

Analog Clocks—5 Minutes

You can tell time if you can count by fives. Look at each clock and write the time next to it. Draw a line to the correct words for each time shown. Read carefully.

Hint: Sometimes the phrase is a little different than time written as numbers.

1  _____ : _____

five after ten

2  _____ : _____

eleven twenty

3  _____ : _____

six thirty-five

4  _____ : _____

nine ten

5  _____ : _____

twelve fifty

6  _____ : _____

five forty

Draw a line from each analog clock to its matching digital clock.

1

2

3

4

5

6

Analog and Digital Clocks

Look at each digital clock time. Draw hands on the analog clock next to it to show the matching time.

1 11:15

2 9:45

3 4:30

4 10:20

5 8:05

6 1:50

7 7:10

8 2:55

Adding Time

Follow the directions to change the time on each digital clock.

| 1 | Add 30 minutes. |

　　6:03　　7:19

———————　　———————　　———————

| 2 | Add 45 minutes. |

———————　　———————　　———————

| 3 | Add one hour and 15 minutes. |

9:45　　　　

———————　　———————　　———————

| 4 | Add four hours and 10 minutes. |

　　4:50　　

———————　　———————　　———————

Adding Time

Answer the questions in each box. Draw clock hands to show the starting time and the ending time. Then write the answer on the line.

1 It is 8:05 AM. School begins in 15 minutes.

Time now  **School begins at** 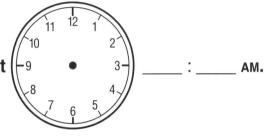 _____ : _____ AM.

2 It is 7:10 PM. The movie begins in 10 minutes.

Time now  **Movie begins at** 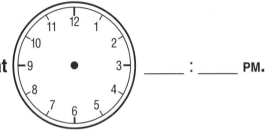 _____ : _____ PM.

3 It is 9:30 AM. The bus leaves in 45 minutes.

Time now  **The bus leaves at** 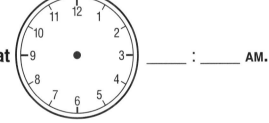 _____ : _____ AM.

4 It is 2:45 PM. School gets out in half an hour.

Time now 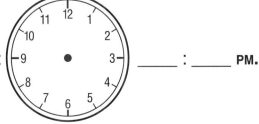 **School gets out at** 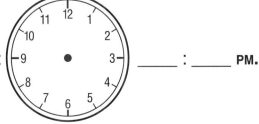 _____ : _____ PM.

Adding Time

Add the minutes to finish each train schedule below.

Train 1

Add 30 minutes.

7:20

7:50

_____

_____

_____

_____

_____

_____

Train 2

Add 15 minutes.

8:50

9:05

_____

_____

_____

_____

_____

_____

Train 3

Add 20 minutes.

8:20

8:40

_____

_____

_____

_____

_____

_____

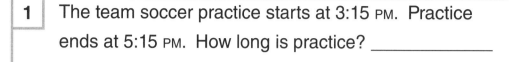

1 The team soccer practice starts at 3:15 PM. Practice ends at 5:15 PM. How long is practice? _____

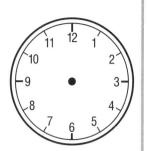

Show the time practice ends on the clock.

2 The school basketball team will be on the court from 4:30 PM until six o'clock tonight. How long will the team be on the court? _____

Show the time the team leaves the court on the clock.

3 Shalom started cleaning her room at 7:00 PM. She finished fifteen minutes later. What time did Shalom finish cleaning her room?

a quarter to 7 or **a quarter past 7**

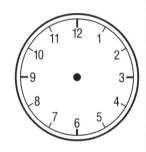

Show the time she finished on the clock.

4 Roberto began cooking dinner at 4:15 PM. It took him half an hour to cook. What time was dinner on the table?

half past 4 or **a quarter to 5**

Show the time he finished on the clock.

5 Jason started warming up for practice at 3:30 PM. He spent 15 minutes warming up. What time did Jason finish?

half past 3 or **a quarter to 4**

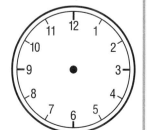

Show the time he finished on the clock.

Solve the problems.

1 The play began at 6:00 PM and lasted 45 minutes.

What time did the play end?

_____

Show the ending time on the clock.

2 Lea's family went to a picnic. They left home at 11:00 AM and arrived thirty minutes later.

What time did they arrive at the picnic? _____

Show the arrival time on the clock.

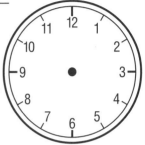

3 Luke does his homework one hour after dinner. If he eats dinner at 7:30 PM what time does he start his homework?

6:30 PM   8:30 PM

Show the time he does his homewok.

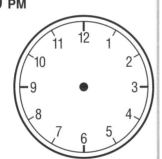

4 Rachel eats lunch every day at noon.

When does she eat lunch?

10:00 AM   12:00 PM

Show the time on the clock.

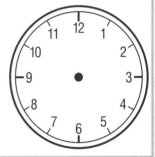

5 Sally comes home from swim practice at 4:30 PM. She eats dinner two hours later.

When does Sally eat dinner?

Write the time.

_____ : _____

Show the time on the clock.

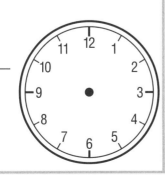

6 Sandy went to the dance at 7:30 PM. She got home three hours later.

When did Sandy get home?

Write the time.

_____ : _____

Show what time Sandy got home on the clock.

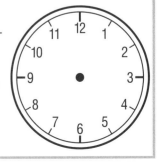

Geometry–2-D Shapes

Trace each gray shape and draw a line to its name. Write the number of sides each shape has inside the shape.

 **1** octagon

 **2** pentagon

 **3** hexagon

4 circle

5 square

 **6** rectangle

 **7** triangle

 **8** oval

1 | Circle the two shapes that are alike.

2 | Cross out the shape that does not belong.

3 | Which shape could be made by putting these two triangles together?

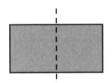

rectangle   **pentagon**   **square**

4 | Circle the shapes that are divided symmetrically.

5 | The teacher drew an octagon on the board. Which shape did he draw?

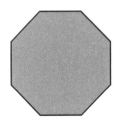  

Geometry–3-D Shapes

---

1 Trace each shape and draw a line to its name.

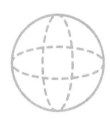

cube   **cylinder**   **sphere**   **cone**

---

2 How many faces does a cube have?

A cube has _____ faces.

---

3 Circle the 3-D shape with four rectangular faces (planes) and two square bases (planes).

             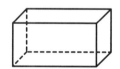

---

4 Describe how the two shapes are different.

          _____

_____

_____

---

5 Circle the shape that is not a solid shape.

          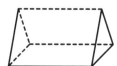   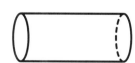

Match the item on the left with the 3-D shape name on the right. Some shape names may have more than one item.

1

cone

2

3

cube

4

5

rectangular prism

6

sphere

7

8

cylinder

Circle the shape that does not belong in each row.

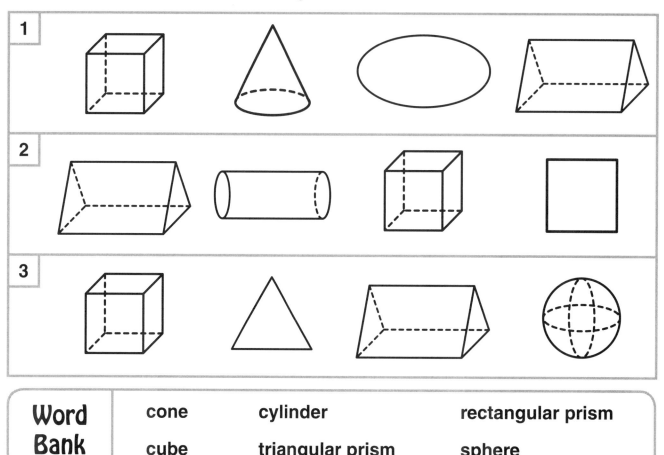

Word Bank	cone	cylinder	rectangular prism
	cube	triangular prism	sphere

Trace the 3-D shapes below. Use the Word Bank above to label each one.

4

_____

5

_____

6

_____

7

_____

8

_____

9

_____

Geometry–Perimeters

The **perimeter** is the distance around a shape. Find the perimeter of each shape in centimeters.

1

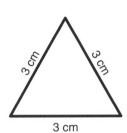

The perimeter of the **triangle** is

_____ cm.

2

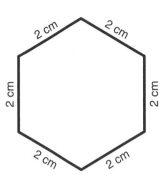

The perimeter of the **hexagon** is

_____ cm.

3

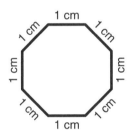

The perimeter of the **octagon** is

_____ cm.

4

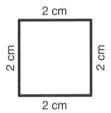

The perimeter of the **square** is

_____ cm.

5

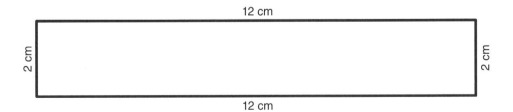

The perimeter of the **rectangle** is _____ cm.

Geometry–Perimeters

The **perimeter** is the distance around a shape. Use a ruler to measure each side, and find its perimeter in centimeters. Then label each shape.

Word Bank	rectangle	square	triangle

1

_____

2

_____

3

_____

4

_____

5

_____

6

_____

Perimeter Word Problems

1 | Mr. Green's garden is in the shape of a triangle. What is the perimeter of the garden?

_____ feet

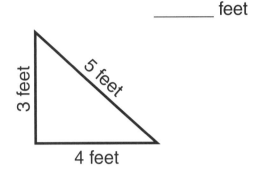

3 feet

5 feet

4 feet

2 | We are going to make a fort. We have mapped out the floor. It will be four feet on each side. What is the perimeter of the fort's floor? _____ feet

3 | The new play area will be in the shape of a rectangle. It will be eight feet long and four feet wide. Mark the sides of the rectangle below. What will the perimeter of the play area be? _____ feet

4 | The Solano family is getting a new pool. It will be an odd shape. What will the perimeter of their new pool be? _____ feet

12 feet

3 feet

2 feet

12 feet

2 feet

Answer questions 1–5. Show your work.

My brother and I divided our room in half.

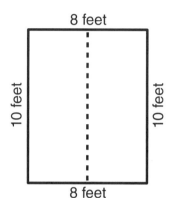

8 feet

10 feet

10 feet

8 feet

1 What is the perimeter of the whole room?

_____

2 What is the perimeter of my half?

_____

The teacher said we could draw shapes with chalk on the black top. I drew a large rhombus. My buddy drew a triangle. Another person drew a rectangle. We measured each side of our shapes and found the perimeters.

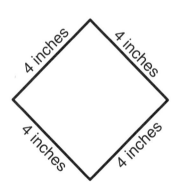

4 inches   4 inches

4 inches   4 inches

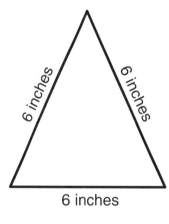

6 inches   6 inches

6 inches

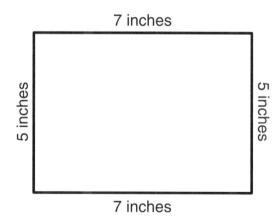

7 inches

5 inches   5 inches

7 inches

3 What is the perimeter of the rhombus? _____

4 What is the perimeter for the triangle? _____

5 What is the perimeter for the rectangle? _____

Answer Key

Page 7

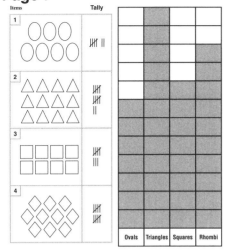

Page 8

Check the graph for accuracy.

birds–17

fish–13

turtles–9

Page 9

1. 7
2. 8
3. 9
4. 6
5. 14
6. Answers will vary.
7. Answers will vary.

Page 10

Check the coloring in each row.

Page 11

Check the arrangement and labeling of the pictures. Below is the correct order.

Page 12

1–6. Check the coloring of the race cars.

7. 5th
8. 6th
9. 2nd
10. 3rd
11. 1st
12. 4th

Page 13

Check the spots on each ladybug.

1. $4 + 4 = 8$ 8. 6
2. $5 + 5 = 10$ 9. 8
3. $8 + 8 = 16$ 10. 14
4. $3 + 3 = 6$ 11. 20
5. $6 + 6 = 12$ 12. 12
6. $9 + 9 = 18$ 13. 18
7. 10   14. 16

Page 14

1. 7   8. 2
2. 5   9. 20
3. 4   10. 11
4. 6   11. $7 + 7 = 14$
5. 3   12. $4 + 4 = 8$
6. 8   13. $3 + 3 = 6$
7. 9   14. $8 + 8 = 16$

Page 15

1–3. Check the groups of ten circled. Check the rectangles around the remaining shapes.

4. 1 ten and 7 ones
5. 1 ten and 2 ones
6. 2 tens and 4 ones
7. 5 tens and zero ones
8. 7 tens and 8 ones
9. 9 tens and 4 ones
10. 16; 1 ten and 6 ones
11. 11; 1 ten and 1 one
12. 14; 1 ten and 4 ones
13. 19; 1 ten and 9 ones

Answer Key (cont.)

Page 16
2. 24; 2 in tens place and 4 in ones place
3. 19; 1 in tens place and 9 in ones place
4. 16; 1 in tens place and 6 in ones place
5. 13; 1 in tens place and 3 in ones place
6. 14; 1 in tens place and 4 in ones place
7. 37; 3 in tens place and 7 in ones place
8. 3; 1 in the tens place
9. 5; 0 in the ones place
10. 12 + 8 = 20

Page 17
1. 4 tens and 9 ones
2. 1 ten and 2 ones
3. 2 tens and 4 ones
4. 5 tens and zero ones
5. 3; 1
6. 30; 1
7. 5; 2
8. 5; 4
9. 20; 0
10. 20
11. 97
12. 44
13. 68

Page 18
1. 6 tens 4 ones = 64
2. 3 tens 7 ones = 37
3. 5 tens 9 ones = 59
4. 8 tens 0 ones = 80
5. twenty-seven
   forty-nine
   twenty
   thirty-five
6. Check circled bars and unit cubes.

Page 19
1. 441
2. 598
3. 651
4. 215
5. 736
6. 189
7. Check coloring.

Page 20
1. 1   7   6
2. 3   9   8
3. 4   7   9
4. 5   8   2
5. 8   7   0
6. 2   8   5
7. 9   0   2
8. 7   4   7
9. 8   9   1
10. 253;   2   5   3
11. 360;   3   6   0
12. 513;   5   1   3

Page 21
1. $367
2. $148
3. $253
4. $532
5. $876
6. $543
7. $28

Page 22
1. 2 hundreds 2 tens 2 ones
2. 3 hundreds 3 tens 3 ones
3. 2 hundreds 4 tens 9 ones
4. 2 hundreds 5 tens 8 ones

Page 23
1. 1, 10, 100, 101, 110
2. 23, 32, 202, 220, 230
3. 35, 53, 350, 353, 533
4. $10.40, $14.10, $16.90, $19.60

Page 24
1. 459; 876; 951
2. 679; 796; 976
3. 455; 456; 457
4. 400; 600; 900
5. 152; 215; 512
6. 687; 779; 789; 899; 980
7. 305; 344; 345; 354; 443
8. 12; 22; 40
9. 230; 320; 450; 540

Page 25
1. 268; 862
2. 127; 721
3. 458; 854
4. 135; 531
5. 113; 311
6. 468; 864
7. 113
8. 864

Answer Key *(cont.)*

Page 26
2. L < G
3. G > L
4. L < G
5. G > L
6. L < G
7. G > L
8. G > L
9. Check problem and illustration.

Page 27
1. F	6. F	11. >	16. >
2. T	7. T	12. <	17. <
3. F	8. T	13. >	18. <
4. T	9. F	14. <	19. <
5. T	10. F	15. <	20. >

Page 28
1. Jane; 12 > 10
2. 10; Tai; 10 > 9
3. Sara; 50 > 15
4. Thursday; 12 < 22

Page 29
1. >
2. <
3. >
4. <
5. >
6. <
7. =
8. <
9. =
10. >
11. 3 < 4; Jenny
12. 14 < 40; Seth
13. 12 = 12; They are equal.

Page 30
1. >	11. T
2. <	12. T
3. <	13. F; 415 < 541 or 541 > 415
4. <	14. F; 423 > 43 or 43 < 423
5. <	15. T
6. <	16. F 21 > 12 or 12 < 21
7. >	17. T
8. =	18. T
9. <	19. F; 210 < 212 or 212 > 210
10. >	20. F; 10 > 9 or 9 < 10

Page 31
1. 28	11. eighteen
2. 39	12. twelve
3. 11	13. thirty-six
4. 46	14. seventeen
5. 24	15. twenty-three
6. 16	16. thirty-four
7. 9	17. seven
8. 15	18. forty-nine
9. 50	19. thirty-three
10. 44	20. forty-two

Page 32
1. <	6. <
2. =	7. >
3. <	8. =
4. >	9. <
5. >	10. >

11. 37; thirty-seven
12. 49; forty-nine

Page 33
1. fifty-seven
2. thirty-eight
3. eighteen
4. seventy-nine
5. ninety-nine
6. ninety-four
7. eighty-two
8. twenty- six
9. one hundred
10. five hundred thirty-eight

79
99
57
100
82
94
18
26
38

Page 34
1. seventy-five
2. eighty-three
3. thirteen
4. ninety-seven
5. one hundred
6. seventy-two
7. forty-nine
8. twenty-eight
9. sixty-one
10. four hundred thirty-four

Answer Key (cont.)

Page 35
1. 228
2. 199
3. 711
4. 556
5. 364
6. 1,000
7. seven hundred eighteen
8. one thousand
9. eight hundred ninety-four
10. five hundred twenty-six
11. nine hundred eighty-four
12. six hundred forty-nine

Page 36
1. 999 → 1000
2. 622 → 623
3. 349 → 350
4. 322 → 323
5. 948 → 949
6. 638 → 639
7. one thousand
8. four hundred seventy-seven
9. six hundred ninety-two
10. eight hundred thirty-five
11. nine hundred twenty-two
12. five hundred forty-six

Page 37
1. 39
2. 47
3. 52
4. 77
5. 24
6. 49
7. 49

Page 38
1. 85 rectangle
2. 65 triangle
3. 28 octagon
4. 20 oval
5. 59 square or rhombus
6. 56 rhombus or square
7. 60 parallelogram
8. 39 hexagon
9. 99 circle

Page 39
1. 39
2. 75
3. 98
4. 49
5. 90
6. 22
7. 72
8. 29
9. 84
10. 56
11. The answers should form a star.

Page 40
1. 70-blue
2. 94-blue
3. 91-red
4. 65-red
5. 100-blue
6. 64-blue

Page 41
1. 48-red
2. 30-purple
3. 61-red
4. 48-red
5. 27-purple
6. 41-red
7. 80-red
8. 42-red
9. 101-red

Page 42
1. 72
2. 81
3. 41
4. 101
5. 90
6. 31
7. 31, 41, 72, 81, 90, 101

Page 43
1. 125
2. 93
3. 114
4. 100
5. 100
6. 143

Check matching lines.

Page 44
1. 143
2. 131
3. 91
4. 97
5. 186
6. 157
7. 123
8. 256
9. 145

Page 45
1. 220
2. 180
3. 140
4. 100
5. 150
6. 174
7. 119
8. 111
9. 170

Page 46
1. 388-orange
2. 945-blue
3. 336-red
4. 796-brown
5. 952-green
6. 663-purple
7. 854-yellow
8. 545-pink

Page 47
1. 253
2. 772
3. 985
4. 341
5. 564
6. 316
7. 202
8. 872
9. 470
10. 685
11. 800
12. 792

Page 48
1. 120 inches
2. 145 inches
3. 171 inches
4. 145 inches
5. Mary
6. Luke and Stan

Page 49
1. 20 + 22 = 42
2. 25 + 21 = 46
3. 16 + 19 = 35
4. 29 + 25 = 54
5. Friday
6. 113
7. 110
8. Ralph

Page 50

12	+	8	=	4		11
23	–	7	=	16		–3
80	–	85	=	25		8
6		19	–	17	=	2

These are the hidden problems.
23 – 7 = 16
80 – 55 = 25
19 – 17 = 2
11 – 3 = 8

Page 51
1. 15-blue
2. 11-blue
3. 15-blue
4. 21-blue
5. 1-orange
6. 7-orange
7. 2-orange
8. 4-orange
9. 5-orange

Page 52
1. 78-orange
2. 74-green
3. 59-blue
4. 28-red
5. 51-pink
6. 29-purple
7. 89-yellow

Page 53
1. 13
2. 4
3. 18
4. 57
5. 16
6. 11
7. Takai

Page 54
1. 2_7_
2. 69
3. 18
4. 39
5. 1_7_
6. 55
7. 53
8. 23
9. _7_5

Page 55
1. 81
2. 94
3. 92
4. 61
5. 82
6. 151

Page 56
1. 257
2. _121_
3. 223
4. 300
5. 53_1_
6. 404
7. 522
8. 82_1_
9. 603

Page 57

Across		*Down*	
A	387	A	345
B	185	B	185
D	592	C	725
F	872	E	285
		G	322

Page 58
1. 248
2. 88
3. 89
4. 480
5. 85
6. 79
7. 218
8. 807
9. rectangle

Page 59
a 696
t 682
i 536
e 85
f 99
r 149
a fir tree

Page 60
1. 36
2. 93
3. Sam
4. 66
5. 33
6. 33

Page 61

1. \$97– \$68 = \$29
2. \$97– \$32 = \$65
3. \$105 – \$68 = \$37
4. \$105 – \$32 = \$73

Page 62

1.

1	2	3	4	5	6	7	8	9	10
11	12	13	14	15	16	17	18	19	20
21	22	23	24	25	26	27	28	29	30
31	32	33	34	35	36	37	38	39	40
41	42	43	44	45	46	47	48	49	50
51	52	53	54	55	56	57	58	59	60
61	62	63	64	65	66	67	68	69	70
71	72	73	74	75	76	77	78	79	80
81	82	83	84	85	86	87	88	89	90
91	92	93	94	95	96	97	98	99	100

2. even

3.

32	34	36	38	40	42	44	46	48
20	22	24	26	28	30	32	34	36

4.

80	78	76	74	72	70	68	66	64

Page 63

1. 6, 10, 16
   24, 28, 32, 40
   44, 46, 54, 58
2. 66, 70
3. 70, 74
4. 40, 44
5. 74, 78
6. 78, 82
7. 86, 90
8. 92, 96
9. 96, 100
10. 6, 8; 66, 88; 42, 50

Page 64

1. 2 + 2 = 4; 2 x 2 = 4
2. 2 + 2 + 2 + 2= 8; 2 x 4 = 8
3. 2 + 2 + 2 = 6; 2 x 3 = 6
4. 2 + 2 + 2 + 2 + 2= 10; 2 x 5 = 10

Page 65

1. 2 x 6 = 12
2. 2 x 3 = 6
3. 2 x 4 = 8
4. 2 x 8 = 16

Page 66

1. 2
2. 4
3. 6
4. 8
5. 10
6. 12
7. 14
8. 16
9. 18
10. 20
11. 2 x 4 =8
12. 2 x 6 =12

Page 67

1. (3) 6 (9) 12 (15) 18 (21) 24 (27)
2. 30 (33) 36 (39) 42 (45) 48 (51)
3. (57) 60 (63) 66 (69) 72 (75)
4. (81) 84 (87) 90 (93) 96 (99)
5. Circle the *odd* numbers.
6. Are all the numbers circled? **YES (NO)**
7. 18, 15, 12, 9, 6, 3
8. 42, 39, 36, 33, 30, 27
9. 3 + 3 + 3 + 3 = 12
10. 3 + 3 + 3 + 3 + 3 = 15

Page 68

1 and 2.

3, (6), 9, (12), 15, (18), 21, (24), 27,
(30), 33, (36), 39, (42), 45, (48), 51, (54),
57, (60), 63, (66), 69, (72), 75, (78),
81, (84), 87, (90), 93, (96), 99,

3. 60, 66
4. 69, 75
5. 40, 46
6. 27, 33
7. 81, 87
8. 48, 54
9. 89, 95
10. 94, 100
11. 6
12. 12
13. 9
14. 15

Page 69

1. 3 + 3 + 3 + 3 + 3 + 3 = 18; 3 x 6 = 18
2. 3 + 3 + 3 + 3 = 12; 3 x 4 = 12
3. 3 + 3 + 3 + 3 + 3 + 3 + 3 = 21; 3 x 7 = 21
4. 3 + 3 + 3 + 3 + 3 = 15; 3 x 5 = 15
5. Check drawings.
6. 9
7. 3 + 3 + 3 = 9
8. 3 x 3 = 9

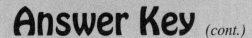

Page 70

1. 3 x 5 = 15
2. 3 x 7 = 21
3. 3 x 3 = 9
4. 3 x 4 = 12
5. 3 x 6 = 18

Page 71

1. 3
2. 6
3. 9
4. 12
5. 15
6. 18
7. 21
8. 24
9. 27
10. 30
11. 3 x 5 = 15
12. 3 x 3 = 9

Page 72

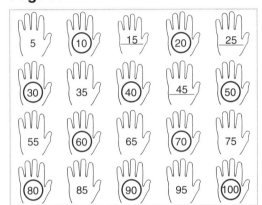

1. 15, 25
2. 30, 40
3. 80, 90
4. 50, 60
5. 5, 15
6. 85, 95
7. 40, 50
8. 70, 80
9. 55, 65
10. 10, 20

Page 73

1. 5 + 5 + 5 = 15
2. 5 + 5 + 5 + 5 = 20
3. 5 + 5 + 5 + 5 + 5 + 5 = 30
4. 5 + 5 + 5 + 5 + 5 + 5 + 5 = 35
5. 5 + 5 + 5 + 5 + 5 = 25

Page 74

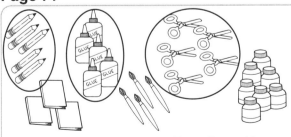

Addition Problem: __5__ + __5__ + __5__ = __15__

Multiplication Problem: __5__ x __3__ = __15__

Page 74 *(cont.)*

1. 5 + 5 + 5 = 15
2. 5 x 3 = 15
3. 15

Page 75

1. 10; 10
2. 20; 20
3. 15; 15
4. 25; 25
5. 5 x 3 = 15
6. 5 x 4 = 20
7. 5 x 5 = 25

Page 76

1. 5
2. 10
3. 15
4. 20
5. 25
6. 30
7. 35
8. 40
9. 45
10. 50
11. 30
12. 45
13. 10
14. 35
15. 25
16. 40
17. 20
18. 0

Page 77

1. 20, 30, 40, 50, 60, 70, 80, 90, 100
2. 10, 30
3. 75, 95
4. 0, 20
5. 37, 57
6. 50, 70
7. 23, 43
8. 48, 68
9. 80, 100
10. 64, 84
11. 2, 22
12. 10 + 10 + 10 + 10 + 10 + 10 = 60
13. 10 + 10 + 10 + 10 + 10 + 10 + 10 +10 = 80

Page 78

1. 10 + 10 + 10 + 10 + 10 + 10 = 60
2. 10 + 10 + 10 + 10 + 10 = 50
3. 26, 46
4. 17, 37
5. 73, 93
6. 34, 54
7. 48, 68
8. 5, 25
9. 39, 59
10. 69, 89

Page 79

1. 30, 30
2. 40, 40
3. 60, 60
4. 40

Answer Key (cont.)

Page 80

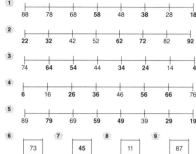

① 88 78 68 **58** 48 **38** 28 18

② **22** **32** **42** **52** **62** **72** 82 **92**

③ 74 **64** **54** 44 **34** **24** 14 4

④ 6 16 **26** **36** 46 **56** **66** 76

⑤ 89 **79** 69 **59** **49** 39 **29** 19

⑥	⑦	⑧	⑨
73	**45**	11	87
63	55	**21**	**77**
53	65	**31**	**67**
43	**75**	41	57
33	**85**	**51**	**47**
23	95	61	**37**

Page 81

1. 10	6. 60	11. 100
2. 20	7. 70	12. 40
3. 30	8. 80	13. 70
4. 40	9. 90	14. 50
5. 50	10. 100	15. 60

Page 82

1. 3 x 3 = 9
2. 5 x 5 = 25
3. 10 x 2 = 20
4. 3 x 4 = 12

Page 83

1. 9 x 2 = 18
2. 5 x 3 = 15
3. 5 x 4 = 20
4. 4 x 4 = 16

Page 84

1. 1   2. 2   3. 4

④ Draw a circle around the picture that shows the fraction $\frac{1}{2}$.

⑤ Draw a triangle on the picture that shows the fraction $\frac{1}{4}$.

⑥ Draw a rectangle on the picture that shows the fraction $\frac{1}{3}$.

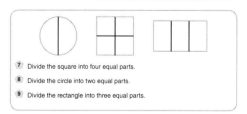

⑦ Divide the square into four equal parts.

⑧ Divide the circle into two equal parts.

⑨ Divide the rectangle into three equal parts.

Page 85

1. check colors; 2
2. 1/2
3. check colors; 3
4. 1/4
5. check colors; 4
6. 1/3
7. check colors; 3 out of 6
8. check colors; 1/2

Page 86

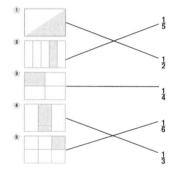

6. 6 out of 12
7. 3 out of 9
8. 1 out of 6

Page 87

1. 2/3	5. 3/5
2. 3/4	6. 2/5
3. 1/2	7. 2/6
4. 1/3	

Page 88

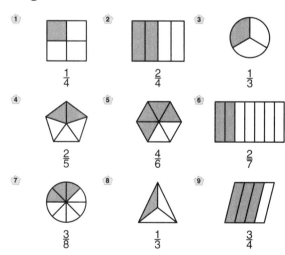

Page 89

Answers will vary.

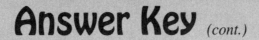

Page 90

1. Check coloring.
2. Check coloring.
3. Check coloring.
4. 3; 3/9
5. 3/9 + 2/9 = 5/9
6. 1/9 + 3/9 = 4/9
7. Check coloring.
8. Check coloring.
9. 5/10
10. 3/10

Page 91

1. 3/11
2. 5/11
3. 7/11
4. Check coloring on bread "crumbs."
Check coloring on sandwich.
5. 2/12
6. 4/12
7. 5/12
8. 1/12

Page 92

1. 5/6
2. 2/7
3. 1/3
4. 4/9
5. 3/6
6. 2/5

Page 93

Check circled answers.

Page 94

1. 3; 3/10; check art
2. 7; 7/12; check art
3. 4; 4; 4/8; check art
4. 4; 4/7; check art

Page 95

1. 2
2. 2
3. 3
4. 3

Page 96

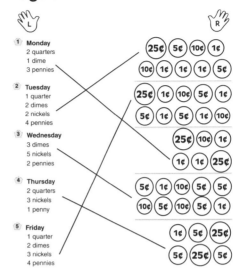

6. Thursday

Page 97

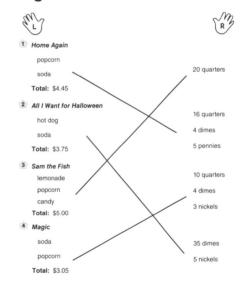

Page 98

NAME	JOBS	TOTAL	REACHED GOAL
Annabelle	walked dog (2 times) sorted recycling washed windows vacuumed car	$4.50	✔
Isabel	washed the car raked leaves	$5.00	✔
Jordan	walked the dog (4 times) pulled weeds	$1.75	
Logan	painted the fence pulled weeds walked the dog	$4.00	✔

Who made the most money? _____Isabel_____

Page 99

1. 22¢	3. 55¢	5. 48¢
2. 68¢	4. 64¢	

Check grid for accuracy.

6. $1.06	9. $1.05
7. $1.42	10. $1.82
8. $1.00	

Page 100

1. $11 − $4 = $7
2. $3 + $4 = $7; $11 − $7 = $4
3. $7 + $2 = $9; $11 − $9 = $2
4. $9 + $3 = $12
5. yes

Page 101

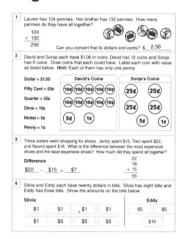

Page 102

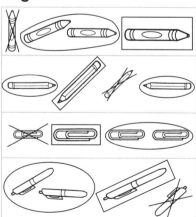

Page 103

1. Check illustration and labels.
2. middle scarf
3. Check illustration and labels.
4. The first and last pencil should be circled.

Page 104

Answers for estimates will vary.

1. 6 ½ inches
2. 4 inches
3. 5 inches
4. 3 ½ inches
5. 6 ½ inches
6. 3 ½ inches
7. 10 ½ inches
8. 4 flags long

Page 105

1. 4 inches
2. 6 inches
3. 1 inch
4. 1 ½ inches
5. 1 inch
6. 2 inches
7. 1 inch

Page 106

1. 16 cm
2. 11 cm
3. 13 cm
4. 9 cm
5. 16 cm
6. 9 cm
7. 13 + 9 = 22 cm
8. 6 cm
9. 13 cm

Page 107
Check plots.

1. 8 − 4 = 4
2. 8 − 2 = 6
3. 4 − 3 = 1
4. 3 − 2 = 1
5. 4 − 2 = 2
6. 8 − 3 = 5

Page 108
Check plots.

1. 20 + 50 = 70
2. 30 + 50 = 80
3. 70 + 50 = 120
4. 30 + 70 = 100
5. 2 and 3
6. 1, 2, and 3

Page 109

1. 4 x 5 = 20
2. 3 x 5 = 15
3. 2 x 5 = 10
4. 6 x 5 = 30
5. 16 + 16 = 32;   16 x 2 = 32
6. 2 x 3 = 6
7. 2 x 5 = 10
8. 2 x 7 = 14

Page 110

1. Mick   4. yes; Check work.
2. Elton   5. no; Check work.
3. 85 – 60 = 25 pounds

Page 111

1. 12 + 28 = 40
2. less than 50 pounds
3. 2 x 12 = 24
4. more than 20 pounds
5. 5 x 3 = 15; 15
6. 7 + 11 + 4 = 22; 22

Page 112

1. Bike 1   5. 20 pounds
2. 38 pounds   6. 27 pounds
3. 57 pounds   7. 15 pounds
4. 71 pounds   8. 1 and 2

Page 113

1. 7   5. December
2. Answers will vary. 6. June
3. 12   7. 7
4. September   8. February

Page 114

1. 27   3. 28 – 19 = 9
2. 28 – 6 = 22   4. 28 – 24 = 4

Page 115

1. 1:15   4. 12:30   7. 5:15
2. 4:30   5. 8:15   8. 9:00
3. 11:00   6. 3:45   9. 7:45

Page 116

1. 6:35 → six thirty-five
2. 10:05 → five after ten
3. 11:20 → eleven twenty
4. 5:40 → five forty
5. 9:10 → nine ten
6. 12:50 → twelve fifty

Page 117

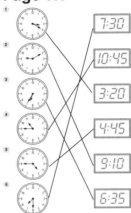

Page 118

Page 119

1. 1:45; 6:33; 7:49
2. 10:56; 9:00; 12:46
3. 11:00; 11:25; 12:45
4. 5:30; 9:00; 10:26

Page 120

(clock worksheet)
1. It is 8:05 AM. School begins in 15 minutes. — 8 : 20 AM
2. It is 7:10 PM. The movie begins in 10 minutes. — 7 : 20 PM
3. It is 9:30 AM. The bus leaves in 45 minutes. — 10 : 15 AM
4. It is 2:45 PM. School gets out in half an hour. — 3 : 15 PM

Page 121

Schedule 1–8:20; 8:50; 9:20; 9:50; 10:20; 10:50

Schedule 2–9:20; 9:35; 9:50; 10:05; 10:20; 10:35

Schedule 3–9:00; 9:20; 9:40; 10:00; 10:20; 10:40

Page 122

1. 2 hours

2. 1 ½ hours

3. a quarter past 7

4. a quarter to 5

5. a quarter to 4

Page 123

1.

2.

3.

4.

5.

6.

Page 124

1. 4; square
2. 5; pentagon
3. 0; oval
4. 4; rectangle
5. 3; triangle
6. 6; hexagon
7. 0; circle
8. 8; octagon

Page 125

1. The rectangles should be circled.
2. The circle should be crossed out.
3. square
4. The rectangle, circle, and triangle should be circled.
5. octagon (first shape)

Page 126

1. cone, sphere, cube, cylinder
2. 6
3. rectangular prism (last shape)
4. One is flat and the other is 3-D.
5. hexagon (first shape)

Page 127

1. sphere
2. cone
3. rectangular prism
4. rectangular prism
5. cube
6. cone
7. cylinder
8. cube

Page 128

1. oval
2. square
3. triangle
4. cube
5. rectangular prism
6. sphere
7. cone
8. triangular prism
9. cylinder

Page 129

1. 9 cm
2. 12 cm
3. 8 cm
4. 8 cm
5. 28 cm

Page 130

1. 5 + 3 + 6 = 14 cm; triangle
2. 6 + 3 + 6 + 3 = 18 cm; rectangle
3. 1 + 1 + 1 + 1 = 4 cm; square
4. 4 + 4 + 4 = 12 cm; triangle
5. 4 + 3 + 4 + 3 = 14 cm; rectangle
6. 3 + 3 + 3 + 3 = 12 cm; square

Page 131

1. 12 feet
2. 16 feet
3. Check marks. 24 feet
4. 31 feet

Page 132

1. 36 feet
2. 28 feet
3. 16 inches
4. 18 inches
5. 24 inches